To –
Gretch
With Love
Callie

GPS

{GOALS & PROVEN STRATEGIES}

SUCCESS for

...from the Industry's Leading Experts

GPS for Success
Copyright © 2011

Published in the United States by
INSIGHT PUBLISHING
Sevierville, Tennessee
www.insightpublishing.com
Cover Design: Emmy Shubert
Interior Format & Design: Chris Ott

ISBN: 978-1-60013-439-5

10 9 8 7 6 5 4 3 2 1

Table of Contents

A Message from the Publisher

O ur ancestors had to go to some rather extreme measures to keep from getting lost. They used landmarks, maps, and the sky to help them find their way. Navigation is much easier today. For less than one hundred dollars, you can get a pocket-sized gadget that will tell you exactly where you are on Earth at any moment. As long as you have a Global Positioning System (GPS) receiver and a clear view of the sky, you'll never be lost again.

So exactly what is the Global Positioning System? It is actually a constellation of twenty-seven Earth-orbiting satellites (twenty-four in operation and three extras in case one fails). The orbits are arranged so that at anytime, anywhere on Earth, there are at least four satellites "visible" in the sky. A GPS receiver's job is to locate four or more of these satellites, figure out the distance to each, and use this information to deduce its own location.

We thought that this system is a great word picture to illustrate the concept of navigating your way to success in business and in life. We've changed the acronym—GPS—and for the purposes of this book, it stands for Goals and Proven Strategies. These elements are vital for success.

The search was on. We wanted to find interesting speakers/authors who believed they had valuable information to contribute regarding this important topic—and we succeeded. Each chapter provides a unique insight into this concept.

I think you will find this book to be extremely helpful and an excellent addition to your library. *GPS for Success* belongs in the home of everyone who wants to know how to navigate the sometimes bewildering path along the road to success.

A rewarding experience awaits you. And it begins with this book.

David Wright is President and Founder of ISN Works and Insight Publishing

CHAPTER ONE

Goals and Passion

An interview with...

Deanna Maio

DAVID WRIGHT (WRIGHT)

Today we're talking with Deanna Maio. Deanna is the founder and president of SavvyGals Coaching and Consulting. She is a professional coach who specializes in helping women business owners to stop wasting time and start making more money. Known professionally as "The SavvyGals Coach," Deanna started coaching in 2005 to help other women get the information, support, and accountability they need to deal with the overwhelming prospect of growing their businesses while still having a fulfilling personal life.

Before starting her own business, Deanna spent more than ten years as a manager, instructional designer, and workshop facilitator in the technology, hospitality, financial services, and professional development industries. She is an active member of Business Network International (BNI), American Society of Training and Development, Association of Psychological Type International, and the International Coach Federation. Deanna is a sought-after speaker and trainer, and is known for her passion and dedication to seeing women all over the world live the lives that they've dreamed of.

Deanna, welcome to *GPS for Success: Goals and Proven Strategies.*

DEANNA MAIO (MAIO)

Thank you so much, I'm so excited to be here with you today.

WRIGHT

So, what do goals have to do with success?

MAIO

To me, a goal comes from a *decision* of what you want. With your decision, you are clear about what you want for your life and your business. The *goal* is then an expression of what you're willing to do to get what you want.

Success is accomplishing goals that create the reality you desire for yourself. But, it doesn't stop there. Let's say you've accomplished your goals or you enjoy a lucky break—it happens! You still need to maintain the results of all that hard work you put in by setting another goal to keep you on track.

WRIGHT

So, how do you start the process of setting goals?

MAIO

I think a lot of people are intimidated by the idea of goal-setting if they haven't done it before. It really is quite simple. Just start by asking yourself, "What do I want?" Figuring this out can be done by having a friend, family member, or a colleague interview you. It could also be sitting down with a journal, maybe on a Sunday morning with your cup of coffee, and just having some time to be introspective. Ask yourself what you want for your life or your business, and what would need to happen for you to get that. It is also important to ask, "What would I have to stop or start doing to achieve my goal?"

Okay, having done all that, now you have a good idea of what you would like to do, what you would like to have, and what you would like to stop or start doing to get it. Next, all you have to do is ask yourself: "What is one thing I could do today or this week that will move me forward toward achieving this?"

Your answers to these questions become the basis for putting together an action plan that you can actually sink your teeth into and achieve. Now, it's more than a dream. Dreams are extremely important, but if a dream is not backed up with a specific goal—something that you can write down, share with others, and work toward—you won't reach it.

WRIGHT

What do you think makes an effective goal?

MAIO

Well, in the coaching industry, and in personal and professional development, you'll often hear that a goal needs to be "smart." SMART is an acronym that supports the idea of effective goal-setting. A goal needs to be:

Specific,
Measurable,
Action-oriented,
Realistic, and have a
Time limit.

When we talk about "Specific," I prefer to use the word "detailed." There is no such thing as being too detailed when you're writing down your goals. It's not enough just to say, "I want to lose weight" or "I want to make more money." Goals really start to take on a power of their own when we can be very specific about what we want to achieve. So, I like to work with my clients by first asking them to make a decision about what their desired reality is—the end result of all their goal-setting. This decision is usually something that can be as short as a phrase or it can be a complete sentence. And, it is spoken in a positive light as if it has already happened.

To give you an example, let's say that I want to grow my business this year. It is not enough just to say, "I want to grow my business." First, we start by crafting a decision, which might look something like, "I have a thriving business where I work with clients who are exciting for me to work with. I get to see them make great changes in their businesses every day, and I'm making more money and having more fun than ever before."

Now, a goal that might align with that decision is, *I want to double my income in the next three months*. Notice how specific I was in this example. Goals are really useful, but the power is in the decision. Once you have made that committed decision, you can set goals along the way to support it. However, the decision always has to come first, and it should be as detailed as possible. If you don't know exactly what end result you are aiming for, you can't have it. It just does not work that way. It would be like being an archer with a blindfold on—she can't focus on the bull's-eye.

Okay, so I've made a decision about what I want out of my business; I've created a specific goal that supports this decision. Now, I need to keep track of my progress. The M in SMART stands for "Measurable." Here is where I see a lot of people fall down or falter because we always need to know if we are on track with our goals. Keeping track helps us stay motivated, and it helps us stay on target with how we are spending our time in our business. To use the example of doubling my income in three months, I can measure that by first asking myself, "How much income do I have today?" I get a very clear number, and then I can track that number over the next three months to work toward doubling it.

The third thing that makes a great effective goal is that it is "Action-oriented." The goal must include a verb that evokes forward movement and direction—something that will actually be taking place. Often, someone will say something like, "Oh, I have a goal: I want to be one hundred and twenty pounds!" That is fine, but that is more the end result you want. How are you going to go about reaching that result? Well, maybe it is "I'm going to change my eating habits" or "I'm going to exercise more" or "I'm going to park my car three spaces farther away from the front door so that I walk more." With these changes, then the goal might be, *I will lose twenty pounds by December 31.* That action-oriented piece has to be in there, otherwise it's not really a goal.

The fourth element is that the SMART goal needs to be "Realistic," which is where I see women business owners struggle in particular. We get clear on what we want, we have a specific idea in mind, it's measurable, it's action-oriented, and yet we set a goal that is too aggressive. Maybe the time period is not realistic, or maybe the goal is too far-reaching based on our current priorities. Women business owners in particular get their hands in a lot of pies—they're busy growing their business; they're busy participating in their community, perhaps they're in PTA or a church group; they've got children and spouses; there is the household to take care of, not to mention the responsibility they feel to be available to their network and their friends. So, they will set a goal that is not humanly possible based on the parameters they have given themselves.

With all these priorities, it is very important to ask: "What do I have on my plate right now?" "What am I willing to give up to achieve this goal?" "Really looking at it, does this actually make sense—is it humanly possible for me to double my business in the next ninety days if I know I'm going to be on a vacation, my kids are starting school in the next week, and we have to do back-to-school shopping?" Also, based on the realities of our businesses, such as the ebb and flow or any cyclical changes, we really have to ask ourselves, "Is this goal actually possible?"

The last piece that makes an effective SMART goal is that there is a "Time limit"—you have to give yourself a deadline. It does not mean that the deadline cannot change as you get moving through the process and find how things are progressing. Perhaps there are challenges that come up—there are always challenges! But, having that deadline gives you something to aim for.

I love it when my clients share their goals with their friends and family and with their colleagues. They speak it out loud and they write it down. This way, they have a little bit of accountability and social pressure to reach that goal by the deadline they have given themselves.

WRIGHT

So, how can I create goals that are right for me and what I want?

MAIO

Often I find people will say, "Well, I just don't know what I want." That is a valid answer. Sometimes, we have so many things happening—so many things that we would like to achieve—that it is hard to pick where we should start first.

One of my favorite tips to offer is to ask your friends and family what they have heard you talking about for a while—something that you would really like to do— and see what they say. It is amazing how perceptive our friends, family, and colleagues can be. They help give us some perspective on what we've really been "noodling" or marinating on over the last week, month, six months, year, or even five years.

I talked with a colleague of mine the other day who said, "I have known that I've wanted to this for the last five years [she's launching a new area of her business], but it was not until someone asked me, 'What have you been talking about doing that you haven't done yet?'" That question made my colleague stop and think, "Oh yeah, this is clearly the direction I want to go right now."

Another great exercise is to just sit down and do a little assessment of your level of satisfaction in what I like to call the "eight key areas of life." These areas really embody our current day or week or month and how we spend our time and energy:

1. Health and Wellness
2. Profession, career, or business
3. Money or finance
4. Friends and family
5. Significant other or Romance
6. Home or physical environment
7. Fun and recreation
8. Personal growth and spirituality

For your business, the eight key areas are:

1. Environment
2. Financial Strength
3. Customer Service
4. Marketing
5. Sales
6. Service or Product
7. Team and Support System
8. Operations and Systems

With these key areas, I have clients ask themselves, "How satisfied am I in each area of my life, on a scale of one to ten?" When you have an opportunity to write down your level of satisfaction in each area and review all of them, go back and ask yourself, "What level of satisfaction would I like to achieve in each of these areas?" This is your ideal. Where there is the largest gap between your ideal level and your actual one? That's a good place to start for improvement. So, say you feel like a "five" with your health, but you would like to feel like an "eight" with less stress and more exercise. Well, what would take you from a "five" to an "eight?" That's what your goal would answer.

When you do this self-check using a scale of one to ten, and then compare the results to your ideal levels of being, you really take stock of what's happening for yourself, both in your life and in your business, right now. That means you set goals that are personal—for you. If you do not have that connection to what you want, then you are just setting the goal because you think that's what you *should* be doing. You could end up creating goals because someone told you that you should, or because you heard someone else set a particular kind of goal.

Well, the reality is that when you don't work for what you really want for yourself, it's not going to happen for you. That level of motivation and passion will not be there when you really need it to enable you to reach that level of success. So, we want to circumvent that and get to what you actually want for yourself.

WRIGHT

What are some of your favorite tips for goal-setting or staying on track with your goals?

MAIO

You may have heard it before, and there's a good reason you have, because it's the best advice for staying on track. It's my number one favorite tip—*write it down*. Write down all the specifics—how you are going to measure the goal, why it is realistic for you, and why that deadline is a good deadline for you. Write it down once and read it every single day, Monday through Sunday. If you have a chance, make notes in your calendar to remind yourself to read your goal.

Let your learning style help you absorb your goal. For example, if you are an auditory learner—you learn best by listening—speak it aloud and as often as possible. If you're a visual learner, read it. If you're a kinesthetic learner and you learn by doing, write it out, repeatedly. There is something really powerful in having the goal written down and this applies to everyone, regardless of their learning style. I recently heard a study reporting that of all the goal-setting tips, this is the one that really effects the most change from people. There is something about how it becomes real once it's written down.

My second tip is to get an accountability partner, whether that is a friend, a colleague, or a member of your network whom you trust. Maybe you hire a professional coach like me to help you stay on track with those goals. Your accountability partner can also help you brainstorm and problem-solve when challenges and obstacles arise that might keep you from moving forward. There is something really beneficial and affirming in having a partner who is standing next to you and cheering you on along the way!

My third tip is to schedule time in your calendar to check in on your progress toward your goal and do the work that is required to reach it. For instance, if my goal is to get more exercise, then I will set an appointment with myself to go to the gym every week. And, if I have an electronic calendar, I will set a reminder for that appointment. Don't give yourself any chance to forget or cancel. Setting goals can be challenging, and you want to make sure you are building support into the process so that you can't flake out on yourself.

To recap on my three favorite tips, they are:

1. Writing it down, reading it, or speaking it out loud.
2. Getting a coach or an accountability partner to help you stay on track.
3. Scheduling time in your own calendar to check in on your progress and to do the work required to reach your goal.

WRIGHT

What's the biggest mistake or challenge you see for people with their goal-setting?

MAIO

Not setting goals at all. Sometimes, people think that if they haven't been goal-setting, it's too late to start or that it's scary and too complicated. Really, that's not true; it is a very simple process. It's a matter of asking yourself: What do you want, what are you doing to get it, and when do you want it?

It is always a good time to set a goal, even if it's a small, baby-step goal. The action can be as simple as this: In the next five minutes, I'm going to stop what I'm doing, get up, walk around my office to stretch my legs, and sit back down. Your goal can be that simple. Then you set a reminder to take a break from your work every hour for five minutes.

It's never too late to start setting goals, and it doesn't have to be complicated. There are many resources available such as using the Internet and asking for advice and support from your friends, family, and colleagues.

WRIGHT

You touched a little bit on passion before, but maybe you could go more into that. What role does passion play in our ability to set and reach goals?

MAIO

It's absolutely critical, David. Without passion for the end result, the benefits you could get from a goal you're not really enthusiastic about would not be very compelling. We most likely will not start taking the action required or even keep at it when times get tough.

There are always challenges to overcome when we set goals for ourselves. A big reason for this is that when we set goals, usually we are stretching ourselves, whether it is personally or professionally. We are looking to make a change, and change can often be difficult. When you have a passion for what you are doing—whether it is getting healthy or reaching out to more clients and making a difference in their lives, or maybe it's spending more time with your family and with your friends—if you don't have a passion for it, chances are you'll never do it.

WRIGHT

How can we discover our passion?

MAIO

It really comes down to asking yourself a few key questions and spending some time—introspective time—reflecting on them.

The first question I would really like to start with is, "What is it that you love to do?" When you do what you love to do, you feel full of energy. These are activities where hours can pass and it feels like moments. What is it about the activity (or activities) that fulfills you, energizes you, and makes you feel like you're doing exactly what you're supposed to do?

Some people call that a mission or a purpose, and other people refer to it as "being in the flow." It doesn't really matter to me what we call it, I'm looking to get to the heart of your activities: What do you love to do? Answer the question whether or not you think you can make a living from it. Often people will say, "Well, I love to do this thing, but I can't make it into a business. No one will pay me to do that, so I'll just do that on the side when I'm not busy." Now is not the time in the process to worry about income.

I was talking with a young gentleman the other day. He knew at a very young age that he liked to argue. I asked him what it was about arguing he liked, and he discovered that one of the things he would really like to explore for a career is being an attorney. He loved the idea of pairing an intellectual argument together with the idea of helping someone solve a problem. So he's working currently in the district attorney's office in our state as an intern while he's doing his law school work.

The second question to ask yourself is, "What gets you frustrated? What is something you wish would change?" Often, the things that set us off actually lead us to what we're passionate about.

The third question I love to ask is, "What makes you laugh?" I find that, often, we are less vulnerable around what makes us laugh versus what we love to do. By "laugh," I mean the physical act of laughing, of course, but I also mean what brings joy into your life? Perhaps it's spending time with young children and helping them learn and grow. These could be your own children, children in your community, or perhaps in your church or the service organization that you participate in. Maybe it's creating something such as a craft like quilting or pottery, painting, or drawing.

When we can ask ourselves what makes us laugh or gives us great joy, we get clearer about what we're passionate about. But, it all begins with introspection—you have to take a little bit of time to ask yourself these questions and then take notes of your responses—write down the answers. If you're someone who doesn't like to journal, have a friend engage you in a conversation about these questions. Really, you get a lot of clarity about what you're passionate about when you do this.

WRIGHT

Why do you think passion is so important in our businesses, careers, and personal lives?

MAIO

You've probably heard the saying, "If you do what you love, you'll never work a day in your life." To go a bit deeper into that, I'd like to ask this: If you do not have passion for your business or career path, what are you doing it for? There are so many opportunities to making a living, why not choose the path we are in because there is something about it that we like, that fills us up, that gives us energy? At the end of the day, what do we feel good about spending our time doing? And this passion you have is not static—things change and *you* change. Perhaps we've outgrown the company we are working for, as we develop as professionals and go further into our career path.

It is interesting that I have clients come to me and say, "You know, I don't need to be happy at work, I just need to make the money that I want to make." I wonder if they say this because they think "happiness" and "work" are incompatible. It's true, you don't need to be happy, but why miss out when it *is* possible for you to have both?

The fact is, when you have passion for what you're doing, somehow the money just comes. And, it is not just financial prosperity; it's also what I call "karmic prosperity." I call it "karmic prosperity" because when we are doing something in which we are proficient, and we have passion for it, things change around you. The environment we're working in changes, and we see the people we work with—our clients, our customers, perhaps the vendors we work with, or our colleagues—start to react and respond, creating shifts and changes. We've become a good example around them for what is possible in life.

So, without that passion for what you are doing each and every day, you are cheating yourself out of the happiness, the joy, and a sense of contentment from using your natural talents. Not only that, but you miss out on the true prosperity, both financial and karmic, that will come to you when you spend your time and energy doing something that you love, and that you're good at.

WRIGHT

So, how can I use my passion and goals to reach success?

MAIO

If I told you that it was already preordained, that it's just going to work if you have passion and you set goals, that you will reach your level of success, it would sound just too easy, wouldn't it? But, it's true! Discovering your passion, putting that passion into a goal, and taking consistent action forward are all you need to reach the success you want.

I think it's important to make sure that you understand what success means to you because it's different for each and every one of us. Also, it's going to change throughout the course of your career path or in the maturity of your business or just during your life. For example, success at one time for me was graduating high school, not that I thought I'd have trouble doing it, but that was a big milestone of achievement I was looking forward to. Then, it was getting my first real job with a desk and a computer and having a regular paycheck. Then later, it was leaving that corporate world and starting my own business. Soon, success for me will be having a business that sustains itself on passive income, where I don't have to be personally involved in its operation every day. So, as your goals and the level of success you'd like to reach change, you can use that passion to fuel the motivation, inspiration, and that sense of empowerment you need to be able to reach that level.

One more thing I'd like to say about success is that it doesn't have to be about business. Success can be raising happy, healthy children. It can be about sharing your gifts and talents in your community as a volunteer. It could be a healthy, happy marriage and supporting your partner as he or she grows a business or a career.

"Success" is a word that we often use without really exploring what it means to us. So, I'd like to suggest that before you even ask yourself about your passions or goals, really spend some time thinking. Think about: "What do I want?" "What does success mean to me?" The answers are different for each and every one of us. Once you get clear on these preliminary questions, knowing what you're passionate about starts to emerge naturally. The goals start to come on their own, and then it all just starts to happen. It's like a freight train—once you get the engine going, inertia keeps it moving forward. It's the same with your goals and your passion—you can't help but move forward after you get the momentum going. You will reach the level of success you desire, whatever it might be for you.

WRIGHT

Well, what a great conversation. I've learned a lot about goal-setting here today. I've written it all down, taken the notes. I've written down "SMART" so that I can understand it: Specific, Measurable, Action-oriented, Realistic, and Timed. That is a good way to remember an effective goal. I've heard the concept before and you've described it in a way that is easy to understand.

I really appreciate all this time you've with me to answer these questions. I'm sure our readers will get a lot out of this. I'm very glad you are part of this project.

MAIO

Well, thank you so much. It's such an honor to be contributing with the other amazing authors in this book. I am doing something that I love. This is my passion and my calling—to help women business owners and the people they influence in their daily lives. I want to show them how to achieve that level of success without the stress, effort, or pain that comes along with *not* using the tools available to us. I really appreciate the opportunity.

About the Author

Deanna Maio is the founder and president of SavvyGals Coaching and Consulting. She is a professional coach who helps women business owners to stop wasting time and start making more money. Known as the "SavvyGal's Coach," Deanna started coaching in 2005 to help other women get the information, support, and accountability they need to deal with the overwhelming prospect of growing their businesses while still having a fulfilling personal life.

Before starting her own business, Deanna spent more than ten years as a manager, instructional designer, and workshop facilitator in the technology, human resources, financial services, and professional development industries. She is an active member of Business Network International (BNI), American Society of Training and Development, Association of Psychological Type International, and the International Coach Federation. Deanna is a sought-after speaker and trainer, and is known for her passion and dedication to seeing women all over the world live the lives that they've dreamed of.

Deanna Maio
Portland, OR
503.922.2688
deanna@savvygals.com
www.savvygals.com

CHAPTER TWO
Speaking as a Performing Art:
Three Presentations "Silver Bullets" You can take to the Bank

An interview with...

Doug Lawrence

DAVID WRIGHT (WRIGHT)

Today we're talking with Doug Lawrence. Doug is a trusted coach and advisor to business executives who rely on him to focus, clarify, and enhance their presentation and messaging skills. His clients include many major corporation CEOs who have come to respect his performance experience as an asset to the business community. In 2007, Doug founded and became the CEO of *Speaking as a Performing Art©*. His articles and speaking engagements are rich in humor and fascinating anecdotes from his career observations.

Doug, welcome to *GPS for Success*.

Before we get too far along, I need to ask you something. As a concert artist, you've performed in large and prestigious concert venues around the world, from Carnegie Hall to the Teatro Colon in Buenos Aires—do you still get nervous?

DOUG LAWRENCE (LAWRENCE)

Everyone gets nervous when performing, simply because none of us can be absolutely sure of the outcome of that performance. If you've been an athlete, an actor, a preacher, or (name your high-level performance area), you've felt anxious when you "step up to the plate," the stage, the camera, or (horrors) the microphone. I don't care how brilliant or accomplished you are, performance pressure is performance pressure, and it's not something you outgrow with age. The big question is, can you turn this "stage fright" into an asset for success? I believe the answer is an unequivocal "yes you can!" So, back to your original question, Yes, I get nervous, but it actually works pretty well for me.

WRIGHT

How so?

LAWRENCE

As I'm sure you know, it takes an adrenal push (adrenaline is one of nature's most powerful and useful hormones) to make it possible for us to go on stage at all. If we didn't feel stressed and nervous, we wouldn't be able to "take" the stage and capture people's attention. It's the energy that comes from this often-called "fight or flight" hormone that allows us to perform convincingly. As a result of this sudden vibrancy, we will appear to be "bigger than life." By the way, if we're not bigger than life, nobody is going to pay the slightest attention to what we're saying or doing. This is a basic law of performing—you must engage people's imagination and thereby assertively get their favorable response to what you're delivering. In other words, people must perceive you as someone to whom attention *should* be paid! Nerves might just provide the energy to make that possible.

WRIGHT

So, are you saying that nervousness can actually work for you to improve your performance product?

LAWRENCE

Absolutely! But, nervousness and how you handle it is just one aspect of my SAAPA (Speaking As A Performing Art©) strategy.

WRIGHT

Would you outline what you believe to be the essential techniques one has to master when "taking the stage" to perform?

LAWRENCE

Well, first, technique, at least by my definition, is what you have to fall back on when there is a sudden surge of doubt about whether you're going to be able to complete your performance task.

As a singer on a world stage with the iconic Leonard Bernstein, I once had a moment in a concert where I just couldn't "find" my voice. The high notes seemed too high, and the outrageously fast moving notes that I had performed so easily the night before seemed impossible at this performance. I panicked! What do I do now (besides break out in a cold sweat)?

This is the kind of situation where I had to quickly shift to my "fall back" position—my basic singing technique—the stuff I learned from taking voice lessons all those years. This is the hard-fought, slow-growth, intensive training that enabled me to be the professional who is paid thousands of dollars a night to sing flawlessly. When an audience pays good money for their seats, they don't expect the performers to mess up their lovely evening. With an expensive meal before, and the rising cost of concert tickets, the expectations are very high. Everyone who has ever "performed" in front of paying customers knows this tyranny of high expectancy.

So, for a few minutes during a performance where I would have loved to have been "expressing myself" artistically, I was actually being forced to look back into my archive of solid technique to get out of the mess that this performance was quickly becoming. Ironically, my nice white-collar "artist" job became a blue-collar "work 'til you drop" job.

WRIGHT

Let me interrupt you for a moment, Doug. The technique required to become a celebrated concert artist is the same as the technique it takes to give talks in front of, say, a Rotary Club?

LAWRENCE

Well, maybe not exactly the same, but there are things these two kinds of events have in common. Here is a list of the similarities that usually exist in all performances whether it's a performing arts stage or a conference breakout session. It's as easy as, well . . . you know . . .

Expectations	Performing Artists	Public Speakers
Look the part!	Must look the part they are playing and create a physicality that exemplifies their role	Must look the part they are playing and create a physicality that exemplifies their role
	Must dramatically seize the room and make it theirs	Must get everyone's attention as fast as possible
	Must "hold" the room through the entire performance	Must "hold" the room through the entire talk
	Must convey nuanced meaning in subtle ways using body language	Must convey nuanced meaning in subtle ways using body language
Be prepared!	Must be completely prepared and rehearsed or they will make disastrous mistakes which, in turn, could create an artistic "train-wreck"	Must be completely prepared and rehearsed or they will undo the value and affect of their speech by misassembling the information
	Must have a strong grasp of the art	Must have a good grasp of the fundamental skills of speaking
Be real!	Must have an almost magnetic charm to engage their audience	Must be charismatic and "emotionally attractive" to their audience
	Must make us cry, laugh, think, or feel	Must make us cry, laugh, think, or feel
	Must convey real emotions based on their own experience or empathy around what others feel	Must convey real emotions based on their own experience or empathy around what others feel

WRIGHT

Again, pardon my interruption—you've listed ten similarities in three categories, are there more?

LAWRENCE

Yes, there are, and I plan to expand on them in a future book, but for now let's just start with *Look the Part.*

I can't tell you how many speakers, CEOs, politicians, and other very public personalities I've worked with who don't have a clue about how to present themselves physically. It's amazing to me that some of these people have been "up front" for years and have never seen a correlation between how they look and how people experience them, especially when they are in a high stakes communication situation. It's all the more amazing since many of them have had extensive backgrounds in debate, speech, and even speech improvement organizations.

Let me cut to the chase here. I often say to clients, "I don't personally need to tell you what to wear, what kind of haircut to get, or what kind of product to put in your hair. You can get that from the scores of published presentation books available." Rather than give clients a litany of the *do's* and *don'ts* of dress (though I'm generally happy to tell them), I prefer this one simple "silver bullet:"

Silver Bullet Number One: Always keep your sternum high. Everything else you do and say will have little affect if your sternum is low.

The sternum, of course, is that bony part of your chest that you pound on when you want to make a point, or, well . . . give your "Tarzan yell" at a party. The sternum is just below your chin and, providing you don't have too many of those, you can easily find it. The sternum basically has two positions—high or low. Actors know exactly how to use the sternum to create the essential persona they are attempting to bring into being. The general rule is that if you are trying to create the look of a loser (depressed all the time, doesn't get the girl, loses the job, etc.) your sternum is in the low position. Conversely, if you are a winner (you get the girl, make the touchdown, marry the quarterback, get the deal of the century) your sternum is high and confident. It's not complicated. If you don't believe this, try the following little exercise:

> The next time you're in a small meeting, keep your sternum elevated from the beginning of the gathering to its conclusion (think Clint Eastwood in a gunfight). Don't say much, if anything. Notice how many times people glance in your direction, hoping you're going to give an opinion. Why? Because it *appears* you

have the answers to the questions being asked. Your body language suggests you know something the others don't.

If you've ever watched *American Idol*, you may have noticed that former judge Paula Abdul always sat with her sternum in the high position. This could be a leftover from her cheerleading days, or it could be the way she needed to position herself to keep from being bullied by Simon. Think about it! She's not very tall and Simon was, somewhat of a bully. Paula had the power to make or break aspiring young talents. How did she make herself heard? Her authority came from how she was *perceived*. Her posture and balance at the very front of her chair and high sternum supplied much of that authority.

Here's another experiment involving the sternum. It's much like the first, only this time you can try it in any one-on-one setting.

Walk (saunter) up to someone you know pretty well with your sternum in the lowered position. You may be surprised to find that the person you're greeting takes total charge of the conversation, and *might* even ask if you're feeling well. If you raise your sternum at some point, you will most likely take over the conversation. "Just do it," as my coaching clients at Nike might say. This whole role-playing switch operates at the subconscious level and has little to do with the content of your exchange.

WRIGHT

This seems almost too easy!

LAWRENCE

The famed twentieth century painter, Hans Hofmann, said, *"The ability to simplify means to eliminate the unnecessary so that the necessary may speak."* I can't tell you how many times I've witnessed speakers who, like a golfer with fifty unnecessary swing thoughts, have so over-complicated their technique that they can't (figuratively) "hit the ball."

Your authority on stage comes first from a perceived idea of who you are, formed by your audience in the first ten seconds of your talk. Believe it!

WRIGHT

Would it be advisable for one to ever start from a low sternum and move to a high sternum for effect?

LAWRENCE

Sure, but it's risky. If your "shtick" is to start with, "I was born in a small town where everybody was poor," and move to, "And when I was twenty-eight I became a billionaire," speech—well, maybe. Just remember, people will make an assumption about your authority from the moment you walk on stage, and it will be their most lasting impression of who you are and who you want to be perceived to be.

WRIGHT

Are there other "silver bullets" under the heading of "Look the Part"?

LAWRENCE

No, but there are some really valuable "copper" bullets such as remembering (men) to button your suit jacket when you're up front. It has become almost fashionable in the past few years to leave a jacket open when speaking to groups. Big mistake! Unless you are at a perfect body weight or less, you just look like an obnoxious and overweight used car salesman with an undisciplined belly. It's like begging people to look at your stomach. Women, to use another common example, often make the infamous horizontal stripes mistake, thereby looking heavier than they might have hoped.

My favorite copper bullet is this not-so-obvious tip. Speakers often bound onto the stage as though they were shot from a canon and getting ready to participate in an NBA championship game. The thought here, of course, is that it's easier to get people motivated if you make a splashy entrance—pump them up before you bore them to death! Most performing artists, however, will tell you that a slower walk to the microphone ensures lots of applause—it suggests that you have both a positive sense of yourself, and profound (often feigned) humility—simultaneously. "Oh, please, all this applause for little ol' me?"

WRIGHT

What's the second silver bullet?

LAWRENCE

Well, under *Be Prepared* (that is to say collecting, assembling, and rehearsing your speech content) I could comfortably boil it down to one thing, because this is the stuff that often gets in the way of an effective presentation—the sin of knowing too much. Let me quickly explain. The so-called "iceberg" principle applies here and often messes up speakers because, instead of focusing on the 10 percent of the information that their audience can and will understand, they start to "drill down" so far that they lose their listeners. I've seen this happen particularly at hi-tech forums where engineers say so much that even other engineers lose track of the content.

I once went to a PhD dissertation "defense" given by a friend who was completing his graduate work at Stanford in electrical engineering. I went because I wanted to be supportive and also because, well . . . there was free food. I told him, following the lecture (and just before the free food), that I had enjoyed his talk, especially the first minute and a half when I still understood what the heck he was talking about. I'm sure that his professors understood what he was saying that afternoon, but the rest of us were swimming in a sea of blissful ignorance.

The point is, never assume everyone knows or even wants to know all about your subject (except when you're defending your dissertation). There is always the possibility that your listeners just don't care! Truthfully, if people are to be interested at all in what we say, we're probably going to have to convince them that they *should* be interested in it. This is basic speech 101—convince your audience. Let me take this in a slightly different direction, however.

Silver Bullet Number Two: Never tell people what you know—tell them what you've learned. This is the only way to guarantee that you will have your audience's attention.

WRIGHT

So, are you re-igniting an old axiom suggesting that information is not as helpful as wisdom?

LAWRENCE

Well, yes, that's at the heart of it. Maybe a good way of explaining this would be to come at it from an artist's point-of-view. There has been, through the centuries, a lot of music written for the human voice. I've had the pleasure of singing most of the repertoire composed for baritones and basses. It's great fun! If you want to turn it into art, however, there are some things you're going to have to do.

Songs always wed music and poetry. Everyone who sings is actually an interpreter of words—a scholar, a critic, an artist. The skill of the artist determines how much his or her audience *feels* about the poem being sung. A really good interpretation of poetry informs our lives at a very deep level and has "stickability."

The "art" part of being a singer is like the "wisdom" part of being a good speaker. Here's an important caution—I may not want you to show me your whole figurative iceberg, going back to the earlier metaphor. What I probably want is the distillation of all your hard work—the upper 10 percent. I actually don't give a rip about what you know—I want to know what you've learned! Why? Because I don't want to make the mistakes you've made—I don't want to experience the pain it took you to get to your "enlightenment."

WRIGHT

Pain?

LAWRENCE

Learning pain—it's the stuff of which wisdom is made. When I'm taking notes at a seminar, I never copy down all the facts—I'll steal those from the PowerPoint stack. No, what I write down is the learning part of the lecture.

Here's a tiny bit of what's in the little leather notebook I always keep with me:

"Live as if you were to die tomorrow. Learn as if you were to live forever." —*Gandhi*

"The best executive is the one who has sense enough to pick good men to do what he wants done, and self-restraint to keep from meddling with them while they do it."
—*Theodore Roosevelt*

"The best vision is insight." —*Malcolm S. Forbes*

Here's another little exercise to prove that this concept of learning versus straight knowledge is for real:

Begin a conversation with a colleague on any subject and dump all the facts you know on the matter into the dialogue. Then, at some point, just stop and say, "Here's what I've learned about this." Watch the body language of your partner change from indifference to actually leaning physically toward you slightly. I unequivocally believe this is one of the great tools of being a good communicator. Trigger the "tell me what you've learned" auto-response.

You can and should create a behavioral objective for your talks. A behavioral objective should be something like:

The group will understand—

The group will be challenged to—

The group will be forced to consider—

The group will be invited to reprocess their—

Creating behavioral objectives like these is the way any good teacher prepares the materials he or she is going to bring to classes. Good communicators have to do the same thing or run the risk of wandering all over the communication map. Telling a few bad jokes, screaming way too much, and leaving people both speechless and clueless does not constitute a good speech. Know where you're going before you start to talk and make sure, before you finish, to tell your audience something about your own learning process. The so-called "application" (speech closer) for what the audience is supposed to do next is often demonstrated in your own personal story.

WRIGHT

Sounds like you're moving into your third area.

LAWRENCE

It's a logical segue out of the last point—I believe the most crucial thing for speakers in the twenty-first century to remember is *Be Real*. Here's a list of the things that we have probably all disliked at one time or another about the many presentations we've endured over the years.

- The mandatory starting joke
- The pre-meditated slaughter of our eardrums for effect
- The "uh, um, eh," syndrome
- The name-dropping, "then I accomplished—wow, look at me," approach
- The obviously manipulative approach
- The "let me say that again" (maybe eight times!) strategy
- The overly humble "I don't know why they asked me to speak" confession
- The overly arrogant "I was able to find time in my very busy schedule" rant

This is only a partial list of the types of speaking styles that have often driven me crazy. It's interesting that some of the above was actually taught in speaking textbooks. Even recently published materials will include some of this remarkably out-of-date advice. It's not that you should never commit any of these sins—they just don't necessarily amount to good speaking technique.

WRIGHT

So, what fits for you in today's paradigm?

LAWRENCE

Every day I see more and more speaking coaches and gurus talking about being "real" and "authentic" when they give advice to people on how to present. In fact, it has become a bit of a buzz phrase for any public speaker organization—"be authentic!"

Allow me once again to take this in a slightly different direction. Have you ever noticed people as they're stumbling out of the airport security area? You know, we're all in the same boat at that point—trying to find a place to put our shoes back on, re-looping our belts, finding our car keys, and figuring out which corner of the tray we should "tilt and slide" to retrieve our loose change. It's quite a study in shame and humility. After all, we're supposed to get dressed at home in the privacy of our bedrooms. This extremely inconvenient security necessity, which makes flying safer is, at best, foolish-looking, and, at worst, downright embarrassing. One doesn't know when there might be a random body search, a biting censure for having a bottle of water, or the awful guilt-inducing discovery that one's boarding pass is buried in the coat which is now blissfully passing through the x-ray machine (I hate it when I do that!). Thankfully, we're all beginning to take this ritual in stride and ignore the indignity.

Life actually holds many situations where we have absolutely no control over how people perceive us. Speaking in front of groups is one of those situations. So, when I say, "Be yourself!" I don't mean pretend you're standing in front of people in your shorts—save that for the airport!

The number one reason why people fear the public stage is that they think they have to be perfect, without a blemish, and totally in control. Otherwise, they will be outed as a total fraud. This is the infamous "impostor syndrome" where you spend your whole life believing that you will eventually be yanked off the stage because everyone will recognize you're a phony. Defenseless and insecure speakers suffer because every little flaw in their presentation makes them incrementally more insecure, until—at last—they disintegrate like an unwrapped forty-year-old Twinkie.

One CEO I know was so busy editing herself as she worked through her annual state of the company talk to stockholders, that she barely said anything memorable or encouraging. Remember the correction fluid White-Out? Her speech was like a ten-page term paper with correction fluid literally dripping off each page. No one in the room could follow her for all the pauses and interruptions. (Incidentally, she was the head of a huge Fortune 500 firm.) In her effort not to make mistakes, she made the biggest presentation misstep you can possibly commit—boring your audience. Mark LeBlanc, past president of the National Speakers Association often uses the expression, "Done is better than 'perfect.'" I totally agree with his point of view, though the overly perfectionistic side of me still struggles with endless onstage editing. I need to get over it!

WRIGHT

Will you clarify that a little more for us?

LAWRENCE

Here's where the speaking "rubber hits the road," as it were. I see speakers (some of them quite seasoned) trying desperately to make the perfect speech. There are a handful of really incredible speakers whose work could be judged as perfect. Most of us should just give up on that dream. If we are not able to give a perfect speech, it's possible we might find comfort in the fact that most people respond to us better if we're slightly flawed. I know one world-class communicator who is so good at what he does that he never gets in trouble or has to take a long pause to recover. I've often overheard people say of his talks that they are phony, packaged, glib, or—worse—trite and vapid.

WRIGHT

All that having been said, what do you mean when you say "be real" when you're speaking?

LAWRENCE

I have observed in the speakers I respect most, a special quality that sets them apart from their competitors.

Silver Bullet Number Three: Nobody is impressed with who you think you are, only by who they actually perceive you to be. Remember, your perception of yourself only occasionally lines up with how others perceive you—unless you are able to present yourself in a fully congruent way.

We're all a little narcissistic. That is to say, we spend a lot of time checking out our reflection in our Narcissus-like pool. The same folly of the young, handsome

Greek mythological character that Sigmund Freud said we all resemble to some extent, drives us to endlessly examine our own worth and beauty. Doing so is not a bad thing unless it absorbs all of our time and energy. So, as we mature, we try to balance our fascination with ourselves with the need to connect with the real world where others exist with equanimity. For many of us, this is one of the great challenges of life.

Performers (yes, this is a confession) often suffer from the pathology of narcissism. To be fair to my fellow performers, however, I should say that it actually takes a certain amount of self-absorption to even function on stage. Most stage performers (especially dancers) spend a fair amount of time in front of the mirror. While doing so, we are not necessarily worried about the specific details of the art we pursue, but, mostly, how others will view us while we are chasing that art. It's somewhat like wanting to be well-liked—but on steroids!

WRIGHT

Oh, I like a good confession! So, artists are a little "sick?"

LAWRENCE

Shh! Very few people know this about us! Just kidding—everyone knows this about us! Here's the challenge—what I've learned—we must be constantly diligent about counteracting the so-called affect of narcissism.

WRIGHT

How would you describe the negative aspects of that "affect?"

LAWRENCE

Quite simply, it causes people to both look at us and be repelled by us. It's like a traffic accident—we know we shouldn't look, but we can't help ourselves. We're so glad that we weren't the victims that we can't keep our eyes off the injured—poor lost souls! The other option to that reaction is that people feel sorry for the victims. In performance, both outcomes are not optimal.

I've seen public speakers who were so taken with themselves on stage that they caused their audience to stare at them—in disbelief. If a presenter seems to genuinely feel that he or she alone has a corner on all truth and knowledge, there is simply no way for us to identify with that person. This lack of identification guarantees that there will be no connective tissue between those of us who perform and those who observe us. Sad!

WRIGHT

Is there a test for deciding what's "real" and what's not?

LAWRENCE

Well, the questions for this test might look like this:

- ❖ Is what I'm saying really true and/or have I given credit where credit is due?
- ❖ Am I speaking from a position of honest conviction or because I think this is what people want to hear?
- ❖ Do I actually have the authority and experience to make this claim?
- ❖ Is there anything I'm intentionally leaving out, and what motivates me to do so?
- ❖ Will what I'm saying enrich people's lives or will it diminish them?
- ❖ Have I exercised restraint in the use of this bully "pulpit," or did I abuse the privilege?
- ❖ Am I striving to leave a legacy of understanding here, or is this in reality all about me?

WRIGHT

You are presenting a pretty good definition of "character." Is that your intention?

LAWRENCE

Yes, and a little bit more. When we speak in front of anyone on any subject, there is an implied contract:

I will give you what is true for me, as I have pursued truth. That doesn't mean you have to agree with everything I say, but I will present what I believe to be true in accordance with your best interests, as I perceive them.

WRIGHT

That's sounds a little "preachy." Did you intend that?

LAWRENCE

Not really. I just believe these are standards against which we are all being judged.

WRIGHT

How so?

LAWRENCE

Going through the world's economic tsunami has created a tremendous distrust in the authority of our nation's leaders and institutions. As a consequence, the tolerance for dishonesty will be slim and none. This will be reflected, I believe, in all areas of our lives—and most particularly in the communication we are used to hearing from people in authority. We will demand the truth, and people in powerful leadership will be scrutinized as never before.

I place public speakers in that position of clout—at least they are authorities while they're up front. That's where *truth* either rings or clatters. We can't afford just to entertain when people give us their absolute attention. Whether our talk is twenty minutes or two hours, people want to hear what's true for the communicator, if not for themselves.

WRIGHT

This interview has taken a direction I didn't expect. We've gone from the practical to the philosophical.

LAWRENCE

For me, it's all of a piece. The substance of public speaking is really all about having influence on others. There is one thing that accompanies the ability (opportunity) to influence people—the need for clarity and positive change. If we can't meet those criteria for public speaking, we probably should not be in that arena.

WRIGHT

I've been speaking my whole life, Doug, and you have raised some things that I haven't verbalized before, but firmly believe. Thanks for reminding us of the joy and responsibility that accompanies the work of being a presenter.

LAWRENCE

It was a great honor to be asked to contribute to this book, David, and a true pleasure to have had this time with you. Let's do it again!

About the Author

Doug Lawrence taught at the University of Southern California, sang in the Hollywood studios in dozens of movies such as Close Encounters of the Third Kind and supplied singing voices for many of Hollywood's biggest stars. His bass-baritone singing career has taken him around the world several times singing with nearly every major orchestra in the world under the batons of conductors such as Leonard Bernstein, Michael Tilson Thomas, Aaron Copland, and Sir Georg Solti, to name a few.

Doug is a trusted coach and advisor to high-level business executives who rely on him to focus and clarify their presentation and messaging skills. His articles and speaking engagements are rich in humor and fascinating anecdotes from his career observations.

"My buddy Doug Lawrence has been a professional singer, music director, and speech coach. In the last forty years, in addition to singing, he's done tons of speaking in front of groups of all sizes. Here's the big surprise: Singing and speaking have everything in common. The main goal is to engage your audience and make them listen to you, so everything a singer does, a speaker ought to do too."

—*Guy Kawasaki, Marketing Sage*

Doug Lawrence
Speaking as a Performing Art®
dlawrenceconsult@mac.com

CHAPTER THREE

8 Gates to Success

An interview with...

Sandra W. Baker

DAVID WRIGHT (WRIGHT)

Today we are talking with Sandra Baker. Sandra is a Master Rapid Eye Technician and trainer, an Intuitive Life Coach, author, and speaker. Through her personal experiences and private practice she has intimate knowledge of releasing emotional pain and stress and has assisted thousands of individuals transform pain and adversity to a life filled with passion, love, and joy. Her transformational sessions and seminars grab the core issue rather than the symptoms and replace limiting perceptions with possibilities. Her products are designed to bring individuals back to remembering their "True Self"—a state of wholeness. She is currently authoring a program called *Awaken the Light Within: How to Create a Life of Peace, Joy and Love.*

Sandra welcome to *GPS for Success.*

SANDRA W. BAKER (BAKER)

Thank you, David.

WRIGHT

Within the context of this book what does success mean to you?

BAKER

My own definition of success has changed over the years of setting goals and achieving them, as well as *not* achieving them.

So many individuals are waiting for a specific goal to be accomplished or event to occur before they can claim success. I believe, as Ben Sweetland stated, "Success is a journey, not a destination."

It comes from the journey of life's lessons of wins and even more so in how we handle our losses. It is through these lessons that we have the opportunity to come to know our true selves. These experiences mold and develop us, if we allow them. Instead of asking, "Why me?" we can ask, "What can I learn from this?" It is through this seeking we can discover who we are and what our purpose on earth is.

Viktor Frankl, one of my heroes, was a psychiatrist and survivor of a Nazi concentration camp. Although he was stripped of all physical necessities and subjected to immense pain, he found meaning in his life through the most difficult circumstances. He discovered success in his journey of the Nazi concentration camp by learning *how to live* rather than giving up. He kept himself and others alive by remaining hopeful. He would imagine seeing his wife again and dream of giving lectures after the war on the psychological lessons he learned. While in the camp, he assisted those who were suicidal. He also gave lectures on health and cared for the sick. He learned how to keep his ultimate freedom, his mind. He was able to meditate and manage his thoughts. In his book, 'Man's Search for Meaning' he states, "Forces beyond your control can take away everything you possess except one thing, your freedom to choose how you will respond to the situation."

Instead of asking, "Why me?" He asked, "What can I learn from this?" He discovered his True Self through finding meaning and purpose to his life in the most dire circumstances. To me this was the ultimate success.

We each can realize our own success in the journey of our lives. We can discover our True Self—the love within us or our God-like nature. I believe our purpose in coming to this planet is this journey of self-realization. As we find this self that has been hidden from our view, we automatically experience more love, peace, gratitude and joy. This is success.

Our authentic or true self is hidden from our view with what I refer to as a "deceptive identity."

WRIGHT

What is a deceptive identity?

BAKER

A deceptive identity is a false sense of self that we pick up at a very young age through programming of negative thoughts and feelings. These can come from parents, teachers, or anyone who may have influenced us. These also can come from our own self-talk. You know that inner voice. Sometimes it is referred to as a "drunken monkey" because it sits on your shoulder and chatters away. It just won't shut up. This drunken monkey is more than limiting beliefs that tell us we're not good enough or that we can't do it. This is negative programming that becomes part of our identity. It feels like our truth. Examples include: I'm unlovable, I'm unimportant, I'm a mistake, and so on. These false perceptions become our reality and distract us from seeing our true, God-like self. This identity takes us further from feeling love or being the love that we are.

Growing up the youngest of seven children, and a twin, I often found myself competing with my sister for my siblings attention. Tammy and I are fraternal twins; she had strawberry blonde, natural curly hair, while mine was dirty blonde and straight. At a very young age, I took on the belief of being second best or unimportant when I noticed her getting more attention. This thought became a belief and ultimately my deceptive identity. I carried it with me throughout my life and it unconsciously affected the way I thought about myself. Anytime it came to competing for something such as a tennis match or even running for student body president in high school, I usually came in second. I assumed people saw me this way, and I self-sabotaged to live up to the unconscious belief. This deceptive identity took me further from feeling love or being love. It took me further from being my True Self.

WRIGHT

How do you measure this success or know when you have achieved the True Self you refer to?

BAKER

Because success is a continual journey toward this True Self, or love, it can be measured by the quality of life you are experiencing now. I simplify this process by dividing it into three basic categories.

1. Career/Money
2. Health
3. Relationships

If you are not experiencing healthy relationships, for example, we would begin to look at all the parts of you that create unhealthy interactions or block you from experiencing love in your relationships.

I believe we are the full creators of our lives, and whatever we are thinking and feeling inwardly, we create outwardly. This of course applies to our physical and emotional health as well as our careers and the amount of money we bring in.

By being aware of how life looks for you now, we put together some proven strategies to create success in each area of your life.

WRIGHT

What are some of your proven strategies to create success?

BAKER

The steps I take clients through I call *8 Gates to Success*. Eight is a number that represents infinite possibilities. The gates represent openings or doorways to your True Self. By moving through these eight gates, you have the ability to experience more love and success. The gates are:

1. Seek
2. Desire to Change
3. Imagine—Create with the End First
4. Be Aware
5. Discover your Deceptive Identity
6. Find the Message of Love
7. Choose to Break the Pattern
8. Meditate on the Go

Seek

This means ask questions. Seek answers to the truth of who you are and what your purpose is here on earth. Our spiritual help is eager to assist us in discovering our truth, but without questions, it is difficult to receive answers. Begin asking to see yourself through God's eyes or the eyes of unconditional love. As I stated earlier, asking "Who am I?" and "What is my purpose?" are two of the most powerful questions you can ask in this lifetime.

Desire to Change

This sounds so obvious, but many individuals are going day to day letting life live them. They are putting out fires, struggling, and trying to make life work. The problem is that they don't realize they can have something else. They don't know what is possible for them. Pain is an incredible motivator. Most people don't desire to change when life is blissful. As problems become painful enough, we seek change. This is when we move into the possibility of choosing to live life. We become aware that we are the creator of our lives and can create something else.

Darin came to see me because his wife wanted a divorce. He thought their life was good and was blindsided when she requested separation. His job was successful, their children were all doing well, most of them grown and starting families of their own, and he considered his life a success. He did not realize how miserable his wife was. Relationships were not one of his strong points and he did not know how to connect to another person authentically. This had never been a problem for him (he thought) until now. The divorce became a motivator for change.

Imagine—Create with the end first

Using imagination creates hopefulness or possibility of something else. Create with the end in mind first. Use your imagination to create a desired end result; this creates clarity of your mental picture. Everything that exists now began first as an idea born from imagination.

You may also use your imagination to choose an emotion to remember a time you felt love, joy, or peace. Most of us, at some point in our lives, have had experiences where we have felt love and gratitude.

I have come to realize that when we want to attain a goal in life, it is really a feeling that we are seeking—the feeling of success or achievement we strive for by obtaining that particular goal. For example, when we want a successful career and plenty of money, we may want the feeling of contentment, security, or freedom to do what we want. By imagining this as already so, you can bring in those feelings of security right now.

Get clear on the end result and as you focus on these wants, the action steps will come to you. When you are able to act out of inspiration to ideas rather than from a fear of lack, you are in harmony with your True Self.

Be Aware

Start paying attention to how you feel throughout the day. These feelings are in direct correlation with your thoughts. When we are able to change our thoughts and feelings, our outer world transforms. We have approximately sixty thousand thoughts or five thousand messages running through our head a day. It would be a bit overwhelming to track your thoughts, so track your emotions instead. A good time to remember to do this is when you eat. Our stomachs tell us when we are hungry, so let this also be a reminder to check in with how you are feeling emotionally.

I created an emotional scale for my clients who had a difficult time identifying how they felt. Rating your emotions on a scale from one to ten simplifies this process. I got this idea from visiting a friend in the hospital. On the wall was a chart rating pain from one to ten. "This is a great idea to use to create awareness," I thought. Except in rating awareness, one represents hopelessness and ten represents joy. A five is feeling right in the middle at okay. This scale allows you to be aware of how you feel and choose to move up one level. Rather than trying to go from a two to a ten, just move emotions up one number at a time. If you're in the lower five numbers, acknowledge where you are and ask, "What would I rather have?"

Discover Your Deceptive Identity

As I stated earlier, the deceptive identity is any belief that stands in the way of who you really are. These beliefs feel like our identity, or part of us, but they are not real according to our True Self. Discovering this false sense of self and our negative, programmed thinking allows us to question them and reprogram our minds to what we would rather have.

We can discover these thoughts through the upsets we have in our lives. Most of our upsets are created from someone or something outside of ourselves triggering our deceptive identity. An upset can be anger, sadness, frustration, or any emotion in the lower five on the emotional scale that says "I'm not okay."

The best way to discover these thoughts is to ask "What do I make this to mean about me?" In other words what is your perception on this story?

For example, James came in to see me for anger issues. His anger was showing up in many places; one of those being on the road in traffic. He didn't know why, he just knew he became very upset when people passed him or cut him off. In session, I had him close his eyes and replay a scene where he had experienced someone doing this to him. As the strong emotions surfaced, I had him allow the anger to be fully present. Then I asked why he felt that way. Underneath all of the thoughts of, "Because he's an idiot and I'm not going to let him take advantage of me," was the feeling that he himself was a loser. Someone cutting him off triggered those feelings he was already carrying within him.

When you can understand what's under blaming another person or projecting your emotions on someone else, you can discover the years of negative programming and self-talk that are being triggered. You can realize your own deceptive identity that continually drives your upsets. Those things you become most defensive about will be a good indicator.

Find the Message of Love

In order to break a pattern, we must honor, release, and reframe it, or choose what we would rather experience. The message of love is designed to do just that. Behind every negative, painful experience there is a message of love—a lesson that we wanted to gain on a soul level for experiencing this pain. These lessons of life mold and develop us and assist us in coming to know our True Self, if we allow them. If we don't allow or honor these experiences, they will continue to show up time and time again throughout life.

Jenny came in to see me devastated because her husband was having an affair. This was the second time he had been seeking relationships outside their marriage. She had huge fears of being left alone and abandoned, yet she couldn't stand the thoughts of him loving another woman and staying with him.

As I assisted her in seeing her own pattern of neediness and dependency on her husband, she was able to understand how her lack of love for herself created so much pain. She constantly needed him to give her accolades or tell her he loved her. As she sensed his pulling away from her, she became more dependent on him.

As we worked together, Jenny could see how she had looked to others her whole life to fill her with feelings that she was loved or okay. This was the underlying issue. She *needed* this outside love. As a little girl, she would perform to receive love and acceptance from her family. "If only I just do [fill in the blank] better, then I'll be loved." The constant need and looking to be fulfilled creates a life of pain. Once we removed her husband from the story, she could see how she had recreated this pattern repeatedly. Her husband's affair was triggering her deceptive identity of I'm unlovable.

The message of love in this experience offered her an opportunity to heal the pattern. Instead of asking, "Why me," she can now ask, "What can I learn from this?" She can begin to learn the truth of who she is through awareness, honoring the emotions, choosing to let those emotions go, and reprogramming her brain to have experiences of being love without something or someone outside herself. She can break the pattern and, as a result, set healthy boundaries.

Choose to break the pattern

The pattern for Jenny was an event triggering feelings of being inferior and inadequate going back to the decision or deceptive identity of "I'm unlovable" and her reaction or coping with this pattern was to make herself loved by doing more for others so they would acknowledge her. Yet she would still feel unloved because the pattern is within her.

The upsets in our lives can be our greatest teachers in letting us know we are in a negative pattern—a self-defeating cycle. Choose to break the pattern by saying, "I am willing to let go of thinking I'm unlovable; it no longer serves me. Instead I choose to be lovable."

In order to break a pattern, it is necessary to have a new experience *physically, emotionally, mentally,* and *spiritually.* The body needs a physical learning to go with this new belief of "I'm loveable." The heart needs to experience the emotion of love coming from within rather than without. The brain needs to understand the pattern. We need to receive a spiritual experience to confirm the feelings of love.

In James' case of releasing anger, he was able to see he was in a pattern when the anger was triggered through someone cutting him off while driving. Being aware of the pattern, he now had a new mental understanding of why he got angry. This gave him a window to choose how to respond rather than react out of anger. He chose a new emotion in that moment saying, "I choose to trade anger for I'm okay." As he practiced doing this, his body got a new physical experience of remaining calm, thus creating a new physical body learning. As he questions who he is without the anger issue and seeks spiritual confirmation of his identity, he is able to get glimpses of a magnificent being who can experience more love.

This process of coaching through upsets and discovering the message of love, is called "Awaken Within." I use "Meditate on the Go" to reprogram the mind using daily habits. Rapid Eye Technology is an excellent tool designed to release the core issues quickly and reframe physically, emotionally, mentally, and spiritually.

Meditate on the Go

One of the most common challenges with spiritual growth and personal development for my clients was their belief that they did not have enough time in the day to spend on themselves reading, writing and meditating. This is why Meditate on the Go was created. It is a program that teaches the "how to put it all together." It is designed to reprogram the mind to create new beliefs that can serve you rather than hurt you through everyday habits.

We have daily rituals we go through of showering, dressing, adorning ourselves, eating, driving, going to work, and so on. Meditate on the Go is designed to create awareness and keep you in the present moment where you are most powerful. It allows you to reprogram the mind by being present to your feelings, choosing your thoughts, and experiencing new emotions of love and confidence. *Meditate on the Go* is not only a concept—it is a workbook designed to go with you throughout the day to track your goals, be the creator of your ideal life, and empower you to make the changes necessary to experience joy in the journey.

An example of Meditate on the Go is while showering, your mind may be wandering all over the place with your to-do list. Instead, practice bringing your attention to the glorious water coming down over your head. Imagine your whole body, mind, and spirit being cleansed of any negativity from the past twenty-four hours. See all that pessimism washing down the drain. As you stand there, being cleansed literally inside and out, allow any ideas or impressions you have been thinking about to come in. This is where a lot of inspiration and million-dollar ideas are born. How many great ideas have you had in the shower? Get in the habit of asking and listening.

WRIGHT

Do you have any other ideas our readers could use to manage their thoughts and feelings?

BAKER

Learn to eliminate judgment throughout your day. It is the constant judgment our minds do that keeps us in pain. We compare ourselves to others, silently berating and beating ourselves up.

Become the observer of the thought without judging it—by imagining a puffy cloud floating by with your thoughts in it. This will give you the ability to observe it and release thoughts more readily. It gives you conscious power to choose the direction of up on your emotional thermostat.

Taking some deep breaths wherever you are is a very quick way to bring your attention to something else. You cannot feel fear while you are deep breathing from your belly. Breathing itself can actually release fear. Right now, inhale a deep breath of air and fill your lungs. Exhale, and as you do, release any negativity, using a sigh to release it. Bring your attention to your breath and see the negativity like gray clouds leaving your mouth. Don't you feel better already? It's amazing what simple deep breathing can do. Three cleansing breaths every hour will keep your thoughts from wandering too far.

When your thoughts seem way out of control and just won't slow down, use an eye patch. This is a simple technique to slow down the brain. Keep the eye that is patched open, this shuts down the opposing brain. This allows the other half of the brain to compensate the shutdown and it will begin communicating from left to right. This is how our brains function best. Patching for even five minutes on each side should make a noticeable difference. This allows you to get out of worry and fear and come to the present moment.

WRIGHT

Can these negative thoughts and emotions affect one's health?

BAKER

Absolutely—our emotions affect the health of our body. This is one of my favorite areas to measure success because our health is vital as an interpreter to what is going on with our emotions. Ignored emotions will eventually show up in the body as symptoms such as headaches and neck and backaches due to stress and tension. Stress weakens anything in the body that is already in an altered state.

Extra weight, for example, can be a way that you feel you need to protect yourself. Subconsciously the extra weight is there to help you feel protected or nurtured by overeating. I've had some clients who have realized that they put on weight to protect them from themselves. They don't want to be beautiful or they might attract a love affair they couldn't resist. Or they discovered they needed to test their spouse to see if he or she really loves them for who they are and not for the size of their body.

Most of us go through life taking our bodies for granted. We use and abuse them with the food we ingest, shortage of sleep, and lack of movement. I believe our bodies are here to serve us. They serve most of us for just for a few decades and then we lay them in the ground.

You are not your body; you are separate from your body. It is housing your spirit and it is up to you and only you to love and care for it. Consider it a gift for you as part of your existence on the Earth. Learn to listen to it. It is constantly talking to you. It may be telling you it is tired, hungry, or longs to be outdoors and wants more oxygen. Is it overly stuffed with food or stressed? What is your body saying to you right now? Listen and act.

You wouldn't put gasoline into your car from a gas station where the sign on the pump says "cheap gas—contaminated but cheap." You obviously know it's not going to save you money because in the long run it's going to hurt your vehicle.

Our vehicle is our body. It carries us through this Earth's experience. What are you fueling your vehicle with?

WRIGHT

Earlier you stated you use Rapid Eye Technology to release core issues quickly. What is Rapid Eye and how does it work?

BAKER

Rapid Eye Technology (RET) is a holistic process trained technicians use to release stress, anxiety, addictions, abuse, and trapped trauma of any kind. It clears negative programming, as well as our deceptive identity. We have the ability to release these beliefs when we're consciously aware of them. RET brings the whole body into a state of balance by simulating our own natural process of releasing through REM sleep, except that we're awake and conscious through the entire process. It's a natural modality that facilitates healing physically, emotionally, mentally, and spiritually. Many veterans have had great success using RET for post traumatic stress disorder.

It works by blinking the eyes to slow down the brain to alpha and theta consciousness. This allows the body to be safe to release trapped trauma. It tells the body to go into a state of balance, light, dark, light, dark, by blinking and puts the brain in REM state.

The Rapid Eye Institute is in Salem, Oregon, and is licensed by the Oregon Department of Education. Rapid Eye Technology was founded by Dr. Ranae Johnson in 1983. There are now thousands of technicians all over the world. You can get more information about Rapid Eye Technology through my Web site SandraWBaker.com and click on "RET" or find a technician through the Institutes Web site at www.rapideyetechnology.com.

WRIGHT

You are an Intuitive Life Coach. What is that, and how does intuition apply here?

BAKER

Intuition is a knowing about things. It is our sixth sense or inner wisdom. It's your own inner coach. Learning to use your intuition will save you a lot of time and assist you in learning the lessons you want in life. Imagine a life where you always know what to do and when to do it; that is what intuition provides you.

My job as an Intuitive Life Coach is to assist others in coming to the knowledge of who they truly are without their limited, distorted perceptions that are creating painful relationships, lack of love, time, money, and health.

I believe we are all incredible beings of love created equally from that love. Love is what we were created from and love is all we are. Anything else that we are acting from is not our truth. However, due to our distorted perceptions, we act from our deceptive identity creating lives of pain and sorrow. As we are able to understand that we are not our negative thoughts or our destructive actions or our bodies, for that matter, it creates an opening of possibilities to see ourselves as God sees us—the love we are. My job as an Intuitive Life Coach is to assist others in seeing themselves from this point of view.

WRIGHT

How can intuition help create success for our readers?

BAKER

Intuition is an essential piece to success. Learning to slow down your thoughts so you can receive inspiration is your own natural GPS system to guide you to be successful in all areas of your life.

Many studies have been conducted on using intuition in business. For example, research done by the New Jersey Institute of Technology studied the relationship between business success and intuition. It was reported that 80 percent of the executives whose companies more than doubled during the past five years had high intuitive abilities.

WRIGHT

What are some steps to create intuition?

BAKER

The following steps will help create intuition:

1. Practice quieting your own "drunken monkey" that keeps you in fear and worry. Do this by the steps we offered above. Deep breathe and imagine your thoughts floating by on clouds.

2.   Ask a question. It's difficult to receive answers without a question. For example: "What is the next step for me to take to create success with my business?" or "What is the next step for me to experience more love?"

3.   Use your imagination to put yourself in a serene place that can fill you with feelings of peace and quiet.

4.   Listen. Many times I will use a pad and pen to assist me in this exercise. Write your question and allow inspiration to flow through you. Write down words or thoughts that come to you. Your intuition will never berate or criticize you. When you hear those thoughts, it is your deceptive identity creeping in. Intuition will be words of encouragement, love, and support. They may also come as negative hunches or feelings in your body warning you about something.

5.   Take off judgment and trust. When you judge what you hear, it blocks intuition from coming in. For example, the judge in our head may be saying, "That couldn't be right. That doesn't make sense. That couldn't be possible." Keep asking for more information and clarity will come. By trusting what you hear, it allows more intuition to flow effortlessly.

As you can see, intuition can create an easier flow to the success we all deserve and can have. As we learn to listen and do the right action steps, we can experience a journey of love, healthy relationships, and an abundance of all good things including more time, money and health.

Most of us go through life believing we have to figure it all out on our own. Not so; I believe we are never alone. We have so much eager spiritual help around us that want us to succeed. We have angels and deceased loved ones who are here to guide and comfort us when we learn to listen.

My husband's first wife passed away due to complications in childbirth. This traumatic event left him alone to raise three young children and a newborn baby. Of course, it completely changed his life. He had to take on full responsibility as the breadwinner and fill the roles of both father and mother. He did this for ten years before we met and married.

Last year he was feeling confused with the loss of his career. The Real Estate market plummeted and he was overwhelmed with what to do. One day he was humming a tune in the shower and asked me if I knew the name of the song. It was a familiar tune from long ago. As he hummed it, he thought of Julie, his wife. She had wanted it sung at her funeral, which was a strange request, since at that time she was young and healthy. The song was "The Impossible Dream," by Andy Williams.

As we played the song and read the lyrics, I received overwhelming feelings of her admiration and respect for him raising those children alone. She knew what he went through. I believe she was with him during his pain and sorrow.

"To dream the impossible dream, to fight the unbeatable foe, to bear with unbearable sorrow, to run where the brave dare not go, to right the unrightable wrong, to love pure and chaste from afar, to try when you arms are too weary, to reach the unreachable star . . . that one man scorned and covered with scars, still strove with his last ounce of courage . . . to be willing to march into hell for a heavenly cause."

My husband, Doug, did go through "hell for a heavenly cause." We all, at some point in our lives, go through hell for a heavenly cause. Although, we may not see the full heavenly cause from our point of view. Julie was acknowledging his sacrifice. The greatest success in her eyes was his raising four beautiful children on his own. She was very proud of him for this accomplishment. During a time of angst and stress in his life, she wanted him to know that he was an amazing man and highly successful! These feelings brought in new hope for him; soon after that, his creativity launched and he invented a new product that is now being sold nationwide. Check out www.mysack.com to see his humorous product.

Be open to feeling, hearing, and experiencing your spiritual help. You are never alone and they want you to succeed in all areas of life.

By following the steps throughout this chapter, you can experience more success in your journey. Honor all of life's experiences. Choose the life you want and create it with intention. Be aware and release the old programming of limiting thoughts that sabotage you. You can recreate healthy thought patterns by Meditating on the Go. They will begin to transform your subconscious to success in all areas of your life.

WRIGHT

Well, what a great conversation Sandra. I really do appreciate the time you've taken to answer all these questions for us in our book. I have learned a lot and I know that our readers will as well.

BAKER

Thank you. It's been a pleasure being here and sharing some of these tools that have worked for me in my life as well as in the lives of my clients. It is my intention that readers will be able to apply some of these techniques to their own life's current situations so that they can access personal power and experience more peace, joy, and love on a daily basis.

WRIGHT

Today we've been talking with Sandra Baker. She is a Certified Rapid Eye Technician, trainer, Intuitive Life Coach, author, speaker, and facilitator. She is currently authoring a program called *Awaken the Light Within: How to Create a Life of Peace, Joy and Love.*

Sandra, thank you so much for being with us today on *GPS for Success.*

About the Author

Sandra W. Baker is an inspirational author and speaker. She is available for corporate and private consulting via Internet, phone, or in person.

Her transformational seminars move, touch, and inspire audiences. She speaks on her processes: Meditate on the Go, Awaken Within, You are not your body, and Intuitive Living. Sandra also tailors her speaking to individual and group needs:

Inspired Living

Creating a Balanced Life

Wellness in the Workplace

Accepting Prosperity and Success

Moving Through Change with Grace and Ease

Leadership with Love and Boundaries

Healthy Grieving: Understanding Loss to Transform Pain to Acceptance

She is a trainer in Intuitive Life Coaching as well as for the Rapid Eye Institute. Her processes and products are designed to bring people back to a state of wholeness.

She and her husband, Doug, have been married fifteen years and are the proud parents of seven beautiful children. They are experienced in blended families, raising teenagers, and dealing with divorce and the loss of a spouse through death. They reside in Highland, Utah.

Sandra W. Baker
4205 W. Park Dr.
Highland, UT
801-628-6788
SandraWBaker.com
AwakenTheLightWithin.com

CHAPTER FOUR
A Values-Based Approach

An interview with...
Dr. Stephen R. Covey

DAVID WRIGHT (WRIGHT)

We're talking today with Dr. Stephen R. Covey, cofounder and vice-chairman of Franklin Covey Company, the largest management company and leadership development organization in the world. Dr. Covey is perhaps best known as author of *The 7 Habits of Highly Effective People,* which is ranked as a number one best-seller by the *New York Times,* having sold more than fourteen million copies in thirty-eight languages throughout the world. Dr. Covey is an internationally respected leadership authority, family expert, teacher, and organizational consultant. He has made teaching principle-centered living and principle-centered leadership his life's work. Dr. Covey is the recipient of the Thomas More College Medallion for Continuing Service to Humanity and has been awarded four honorary doctorate degrees. Other awards given Dr. Covey include the Sikh's 1989 International Man of Peace award, the 1994 International Entrepreneur of the Year award, *Inc.* magazine's Services Entrepreneur of the Year award, and in 1996 the National Entrepreneur of the Year Lifetime Achievement award for Entrepreneurial leadership. He has also been recognized as one of *Time* magazine's twenty-five most influential Americans and one of *Sales and Marketing Management's* top twenty-five power brokers. As the father of nine and grandfather of forty-four, Dr. Covey received the 2003 National Fatherhood Award, which he says is the most meaningful award he has ever received. Dr. Covey earned his undergraduate degree from the University of Utah, his MBA from Harvard, and completed his doctorate at Brigham Young University. While at Brigham Young he served as assistant to the

President and was also a professor of Business Management and Organizational Behavior.

Dr. Covey, welcome to *GPS for Success: Goals and Proven Strategies.*

DR. STEPHEN COVEY (COVEY)

Thank you.

WRIGHT

Dr. Covey, most companies make decisions and filter them down through their organization. You, however, state that no company can succeed until individuals within it succeed. Are the goals of the company the result of the combined goals of the individuals?

COVEY

Absolutely—if people aren't on the same page, they're going to be pulling in different directions. To teach this concept, I frequently ask large audiences to close their eyes and point north, and then to keep pointing and open their eyes. They find themselves pointing all over the place. I say to them, "Tomorrow morning if you want a similar experience, ask the first ten people you meet in your organization what the purpose of your organization is and you'll find it's a very similar experience. They'll point all over the place." When people have a different sense of purpose and values, every decision that is made from then on is governed by those. There's no question that this is one of the fundamental causes of misalignment, low trust, interpersonal conflict, interdepartmental rivalry, people operating on personal agendas, and so forth.

WRIGHT

Is that primarily a result of an inability to communicate from the top?

COVEY

That's one aspect, but I think it's more fundamental. There's an inability to involve people—an unwillingness. Leaders may communicate what their mission and their strategy is, but that doesn't mean there's any emotional connection to it. Mission statements that are rushed and then announced are soon forgotten. They become nothing more than just a bunch of platitudes on the wall that mean essentially nothing and even create a source of cynicism and a sense of hypocrisy inside the culture of an organization.

WRIGHT

How do companies ensure survival and prosperity in these tumultuous times of technological advances, mergers, downsizing, and change?

COVEY

I think that it takes a lot of high trust in a culture that has something that doesn't change—principles—at its core. There are principles that people agree upon that are valued. It gives a sense of stability. Then you have the power to adapt and be flexible when you experience these kinds of disruptive new economic models or technologies that come in and sideswipe you. You don't know how to handle them unless you have something you can depend upon.

If people have not agreed to a common set of principles that guide them and a common purpose, then they get their security from the outside and they tend to freeze the structure, systems, and processes inside and they cease becoming adaptable. They don't change with the changing realities of the new marketplace out there and gradually they become obsolete.

WRIGHT

I was interested in one portion of your book, *The 7 Habits of Highly Effective People,* where you talk about behaviors. How does an individual go about the process of replacing ineffective behaviors with effective ones?

COVEY

I think that for most people it usually requires a crisis that humbles them to become aware of their ineffective behaviors. If there's not a crisis the tendency is to perpetuate those behaviors and not change.

You don't have to wait until the marketplace creates the crisis for you. Have everyone accountable on a 360-degree basis to everyone else they interact with—with feedback either formal or informal—where they are getting data as to what's happening. They will then start to realize that the consequences of their ineffective behavior require them to be humble enough to look at that behavior and to adopt new, more effective ways of doing things.

Sometimes people can be stirred up to this if you just appeal to their conscience—to their inward sense of what is right and wrong. A lot of people sometimes know inwardly they're doing wrong, but the culture doesn't necessarily discourage them from continuing that. They either need feedback from people or they need feedback from the marketplace or they need feedback from their conscience. Then they can begin to develop a step-by-step process of replacing old habits with new, better habits.

WRIGHT

It's almost like saying, "Let's make all the mistakes in the laboratory before we put this thing in the air."

COVEY

Right; and I also think what is necessary is a paradigm shift, which is analogous to having a correct map, say of a city or of a country. If people have an inaccurate paradigm of life, of other people, and of themselves it really doesn't make much difference what their behavior or habits or attitudes are. What they need is a correct paradigm—a correct map—that describes what's going on.

For instance, in the Middle Ages they used to heal people through bloodletting. It wasn't until Samuel Weiss and Pasteur and other empirical scientists discovered the germ theory that they realized for the first time they weren't dealing with the real issue. They realized why women preferred to use midwives who washed rather than doctors who didn't wash. They gradually got a new paradigm. Once you've got a new paradigm then your behavior and your attitude flow directly from it. If you have a bad paradigm or a bad map, let's say of a city, there's no way, no matter what your behavior or your habits or your attitudes are—how positive they are—you'll never be able to find the location you're looking for. This is why I believe that to change paradigms is far more fundamental than to work on attitude and behavior.

WRIGHT

One of your seven habits of highly effective people is to "begin with the end in mind." If circumstances change and hardships or miscalculations occur, how does one view the end with clarity?

COVEY

Many people think to begin with the end in mind means that you have some fixed definition of a goal that's accomplished and if changes come about you're not going to adapt to them. Instead, the "end in mind" you begin with is that you are going to create a flexible culture of high trust so that no matter what comes along you are going to do whatever it takes to accommodate that new change or that new reality and maintain a culture of high performance and high trust. You're talking more in terms of values and overall purposes that don't change, rather than specific strategies or programs that will have to change to accommodate the changing realities in the marketplace.

WRIGHT

In this time of mistrust among people, corporations, and nations, for that matter, how do we create high levels of trust?

COVEY

That's a great question and it's complicated because there are so many elements that go into the creating of a culture of trust. Obviously the most fundamental one is just to have trustworthy people. But that is not sufficient because what if the organization itself is misaligned?

For instance, what if you say you value cooperation but you really reward people for internal competition? Then you have a systemic or a structure problem that creates low trust inside the culture even though the people themselves are trustworthy. This is one of the insights of Edward Demming and the work he did. That's why he said that most problems are not personal—they're systemic. They're common caused. That's why you have to work on structure, systems, and processes to make sure that they institutionalize principle-centered values. Otherwise you could have good people with bad systems and you'll get bad results.

When it comes to developing interpersonal trust between people, it is made up of many, many elements such as taking the time to listen to other people, to understand them, and to see what is important to them. What we think is important to another may only be important to us, not to another. It takes empathy. You have to make and keep promises to them. You have to treat people with kindness and courtesy. You have to be completely honest and open. You have to live up to your commitments. You can't betray people behind their back. You can't badmouth them behind their back and sweet-talk them to their face. That will send out vibes of hypocrisy and it will be detected.

You have to learn to apologize when you make mistakes, to admit mistakes, and to also get feedback going in every direction as much as possible. It doesn't necessarily require formal forums—it requires trust between people who will be open with each other and give each other feedback.

WRIGHT

My mother told me to do a lot of what you're saying now, but it seems that when I got in business I simply forgot.

COVEY

Sometimes we forget, but sometimes culture doesn't nurture it. That's why I say unless you work with the institutionalizing—that means formalizing into structure, systems, and processing the values—you will not have a nurturing culture. You have to constantly work on that.

This is one of the big mistakes organizations make. They think trust is simply a function of being honest. That's only one small aspect. It's an important aspect, obviously, but there are so many other elements that go into the creation of a high-trust culture.

WRIGHT

"Seek first to understand then to be understood" is another of your seven habits. Do you find that people try to communicate without really understanding what other people want?

COVEY

Absolutely. The tendency is to project out of our own autobiography—our own life, our own value system—onto other people, thinking we know what they want. So we don't really listen to them. We pretend to listen, but we really don't listen from within their frame of reference. We listen from within our own frame of reference and we're really preparing our reply rather than seeking to understand. This is a very common thing. In fact, very few people have had any training in seriously listening. They're trained in how to read, write, and speak, but not to listen.

Reading, writing, speaking, and listening are the four modes of communication and they represent about two-thirds to three-fourths of our waking hours. About half of that time is spent listening, but it's the one skill people have not been trained in. People have had all this training in the other forms of communication. In a large audience of 1,000 people you wouldn't have more than twenty people who have had more than two weeks of training in listening. Listening is more than a skill or technique; you must listen within another's frame of reference. It takes tremendous courage to listen because you're at risk when you listen. You don't know what's going to happen; you're vulnerable.

WRIGHT

Sales gurus always tell me that the number one skill in selling is listening.

COVEY

Yes—listening from within the customer's frame of reference. That is so true. You can see that it takes some security to do that because you don't know what's going to happen.

WRIGHT

With this book we're trying to encourage people to be better, to live better, and be more fulfilled by listening to the examples of our guest authors. Is there anything or anyone in your life that has made a difference for you and helped you to become a better person?

COVEY

I think the most influential people in my life have been my parents. I think that what they modeled was not to make comparisons and harbor jealousy or to seek recognition. They were humble people.

I remember one time when my mother and I were going up in an elevator and the most prominent person in the state was also in the elevator. She knew him, but she spent her time talking to the elevator operator. I was just a little kid and I was so awed by the famous person. I said to her, "Why didn't you talk to the important person?" She said, "I was. I had never met him."

My parents were really humble, modest people who were focused on service and other people rather than on themselves. I think they were very inspiring models to me.

WRIGHT

In almost every research paper I've ever read, those who write about people who have influenced their lives include three teachers in their top-five picks. My seventh-grade English teacher was the greatest teacher I ever had and she influenced me to no end.

COVEY

Would it be correct to say that she saw in you probably some qualities of greatness you didn't even see in yourself?

WRIGHT

Absolutely.

COVEY

That's been my general experience—the key aspect of a mentor or a teacher is someone who sees in you potential that you don't even see in yourself. Those teachers/mentors treat you accordingly and eventually you come to see it in yourself. That's my definition of leadership or influence—communicating people's worth and potential so clearly that they are inspired to see it in themselves.

WRIGHT

Most of my teachers treated me as a student, but she treated me with much more respect than that. As a matter of fact, she called me Mr. Wright, and I was in the seventh grade at the time. I'd never been addressed by anything but a nickname. I stood a little taller; she just made a tremendous difference.

Do you think there are other characteristics that mentors seem to have in common?

COVEY

I think they are first of all good examples in their own personal lives. Their personal lives and their family lives are not all messed up—they come from a base of good character. They also are usually very confident and they take the time to do what your teacher did to you—to treat you with uncommon respect and courtesy.

They also, I think, explicitly teach principles rather than practices so that rules don't take the place of human judgment. You gradually come to have faith in your own judgment in making decisions because of the affirmation of such a mentor.

Good mentors care about you—you can feel the sincerity of their caring. It's like the expression, "I don't care how much you know until I know how much you care."

WRIGHT

Most people are fascinated with the new television shows about being a survivor. What has been the greatest comeback that you've made from adversity in your career or your life?

COVEY

When I was in grade school I experienced a disease in my legs. It caused me to use crutches for a while. I tried to get off them fast and get back. The disease wasn't corrected yet so I went back on crutches for another year. The disease went to the other leg and I went on for another year. It essentially took me out of my favorite thing—athletics—and it took me more into being a student. So that was a life-defining experience, which at the time seemed very negative, but has proven to be the basis on which I've focused my life—being more of a learner.

WRIGHT

Principle-centered learning is basically what you do that's different from anybody I've read or listened to.

COVEY

The concept is embodied in the Far Eastern expression, "Give a man a fish, you feed him for the day; teach him how to fish, you feed him for a lifetime." When you teach principles that are universal and timeless, they don't belong to just any one person's religion or to a particular culture or geography. They seem to be timeless and universal like the ones we've been talking about here: trustworthiness, honesty, caring, service, growth, and development. These are universal principles. If you focus on these things, then little by little people become independent of you and then they start to believe in themselves and their own judgment becomes better. You don't need as many rules. You don't need as much bureaucracy and as many controls and you can empower people.

The problem in most business operations today—and not just business but non-business—is that they're using the industrial model in an information age. Arnold Toynbee, the great historian, said, "You can pretty well summarize all of history in four words: nothing fails like success." The industrial model was based on the asset of the machine. The information model is based on the asset of the person—the knowledge worker. It's an altogether different model. But the machine model was the main asset of the twentieth century. It enabled productivity to increase fifty times. The new asset is intellectual and social capital—the qualities of people and the quality of the relationship they have with each other. Like Toynbee said, "Nothing fails like success." The industrial model does not work in an information age. It requires a focus on the new wealth, not capital and material things.

A good illustration that demonstrates how much we were into the industrial model, and still are, is to notice where people are on the balance sheet. They're not found there. Machines are found there. Machines become investments. People are on the profit-and-loss statement and people are expenses. Think of that—if that isn't bloodletting.

WRIGHT

It sure is.

When you consider the choices you've made down through the years, has faith played an important role in your life?

COVEY

It has played an extremely important role. I believe deeply that we should put principles at the center of our lives, but I believe that God is the source of those principles. I did not invent them. I get credit sometimes for some of the Seven Habits material and some of the other things I've done, but it's really all based on principles that have been given by God to all of His children from the beginning of time. You'll find that you can teach these same principles from the sacred texts and the wisdom literature of almost any tradition. I think the ultimate source of that is God and that is one thing you can absolutely depend upon—"in God we trust."

WRIGHT

If you could have a platform and tell our audience something you feel would help them or encourage them, what would you say?

COVEY

I think I would say to put God at the center of your life and then prioritize your family. No one on their deathbed ever wished they had spent more time at the office.

WRIGHT

That's right. We have come down to the end of our program and I know you're a busy person. I could talk with you all day, Dr. Covey.

COVEY

It's good to talk with you as well and to be a part of this program. It looks like an excellent one that you've got going on here.

WRIGHT

Thank you.

We have been talking today with Dr. Stephen R. Covey, cofounder and vice-chairman of Franklin Covey Company. He's also the author of *The 7 Habits of Highly Effective People,* which has been ranked as a number one bestseller by the *New York Times*, selling more than fourteen million copies in thirty-eight languages.

Dr. Covey, thank you so much for being with us today.

COVEY

Thank you for the honor of participating.

ABOUT THE AUTHOR

Stephen R. Covey was recognized in 1996 as one of *Time* magazine's twenty-five most influential Americans and one of *Sales and Marketing Management's* top twenty-five power brokers. Dr. Covey is the author of several acclaimed books, including the international bestseller, *The 7 Habits of Highly Effective People*, named the number one Most Influential Business Book of the Twentieth Century, and other best sellers that include *First Things First, Principle-Centered Leadership,* (with sales exceeding one million) and *The 7 Habits of Highly Effective Families.*

Dr. Covey's newest book, *The 8th Habit: From Effectiveness to Greatness*, which was released in November 2004, rose to the top of several bestseller lists, including *New York Times, Wall Street Journal, USA Today, Money, Business Week*, Amazon.com, and Barnes & Noble.

Dr. Covey currently serves on the board of directors for the Points of Light Foundation. Based in Washington, D.C., the Foundation, through its partnership with the Volunteer Center National Network, engages and mobilizes millions of volunteers from all walks of life—businesses, nonprofits, faith-based organizations, low-income communities, families, youth, and older adults—to help

Dr. Stephen R. Covey
www.stephencovey.com

CHAPTER FIVE

Propel Your Marketing Forward

An interview with...

Richard Martin

DAVID WRIGHT (WRIGHT)

Today we're talking with Richard Martin. Richard is the Chief Catalyst of International Business Fuel. He began his career in the United States Army where he was an honor graduate from both the Army Ranger School and the Special Forces Qualifications Course. Now he works with entrepreneurs, business owners, sales teams, and professionals creating entrepreneurial success. As an entrepreneurial leadership expert specializing in business growth, Rich helps business people connect with their passion and people to generate profits. He is the developer of the Business Propellant training program and the Catalyst Groups concept. His fast-paced, results-driven seminars have built him the reputation as a trainer who maximizes what everyone takes away.

Rich Martin, welcome to *GPS for Success.*

RICHARD MARTIN (MARTIN)

Well, I'm glad to be here, thank you.

WRIGHT

Why do you consider marketing to be so crucial to the success of a business?

MARTIN

Well, David, it's interesting—if you think about it, a business really isn't doing business unless it has customers. To me, marketing is how businesses plan to get customers. So marketing really is central to the idea of a business plan or business, in my mind. Marketing is the essential piece, though, that makes it all happen; marketing is what actually puts you in business. So when entrepreneurs come to me, or when I'm working with someone on a business plan, I feel it's most important for them to put a marketing plan together and to figure out how they're going to get customers. We've all heard the saying—build a better mousetrap and they'll beat the doors down trying to get to it. Well, it's not true. You can have that better mousetrap and unless people know about it, they will never come walking through your door to buy it, let alone beat the doors down.

I'm really sold that marketing is the most important part of business because marketing is getting the word out to customers; marketing lets your customers know what you have to offer. Without actually making sales, you're not in business. Marketing is what enables businesses to make sales.

WRIGHT

Many of us have heard that there is a "best" form of marketing all businesses can employ. What could you tell our readers about this form of marketing?

MARTIN

That is an interesting question. It's a very interesting question because if you asked people who are in business, "What's the best way to get customers?" they'll tell you "word-of-mouth." In fact, most will say that's an easy answer. They all say it proudly, "Well, gosh, that's easy—it's word-of-mouth." Then if you ask them (and I've done this with quite a few businesspeople now), "How do you get word-of-mouth business?" they will stand there and look at you.

Some of them will throw some answers out, but few have ever been exposed to a well thought-out strategic plan to build their business by "word-of-mouth." In fact, this is the very reason Dr. Ivan Misner, Founder of BNI and the Referral Institute, wrote the book *World's Best Known Marketing Secret*. Everyone seems to know that word-of-mouth is the best way to get business, but how to make it work certainly seemed to be a secret.

Word-of-mouth referrals are the absolute best way to get business—to market your business—because when you get word-of-mouth or referrals to people, they have already more or less decided to use your service by the time they contact you. They're already in the market, they're already looking for what you have, and they come to your door for a solution to a problem that they have. So word-of-mouth referrals just really make sense—they keep your overhead down, you get a more profitable customer, and people who come through word-of-mouth are not as price-driven. They are the best customer that you can get, in my opinion and in just about everybody's opinion. In fact, just recently, all the Fortune 500 companies started taking notice of word-of-mouth marketing. They're figuring out how they can go about activating it on a larger level. It clearly stands out in the marketing world as the most efficient way to market.

WRIGHT

How does word-of-mouth marketing work? We've all heard of it, but doesn't word-of-mouth just happen when a business has great customer service?

MARTIN

Yes, that is what everyone thinks, but it simply isn't true. Think about it—think about going out and doing business with someone you currently shop with or a business that has provided great customer service. Now think about doing business somewhere that didn't or doesn't have great customer service. Which one did you go back to? You went back to the one that had great customer service, right?

WRIGHT

Right.

MARTIN

If the business didn't have great customer service you didn't go back at all, did you?

WRIGHT

You've got that right.

MARTIN

So, great customer service is a prerequisite to being in business. If you don't have great customer service, you may be able to sustain yourself for a while simply through advertising and getting new customers, but you'll not get repeat business and you'll never get people to talk about your business.

The greatest fallacy is that if a business has great customer service, customers and clients are going to go out and tell everybody about that business. There have been some studies done on this, and the fact is that if people get great customer service, they may tell one or two people about it. Unless it's absolutely outrageously crazy good customer service, customers and clients will only tell one or two people about it. Now, on the other hand (as I understand it), in the case of bad customer service, the average person goes out and tells ten people. So customer word-of-mouth on the subject of customer service is actually weighted toward the negative. You can easily generate a huge amount of negative word-of-mouth and publicity for your business by not having great customer service, but great customer service really doesn't generate much at all in comparison.

Word-of-mouth marketing works based on relationships—relationships that you have with customers, relationships that you have with suppliers, relationships that you have with referral sources. In fact, there are many sources of referrals. Specifically, there are eight different sources of referrals as defined by the Referral Institute, a training company that trains the complete process of building word-of-mouth marketing plans. There are eight sources, of referrals and customers are only one of those. Word-of-mouth works because of these relationships and is based on the fact that after you have a deep relationship, you can ask for the referrals. I've known many people who have built good relationships and have not asked for business. They have not sat down and asked, "How can I help you with your business?" and then at one point asked, "Okay, how can you help me with my business?" The referrals come from asking.

Another point I would like to emphasize is that referrals are really based on relationships. One of the first pieces I read about marketing after I got into business was by a gentleman named Jay Abraham. He says that the best time to ask for a referral is right when someone does business with you. When you go out and buy something, aren't you making a decision to trust that business enough to let it solve a problem you have? You certainly are. You trust that business at that moment because that's when you have that problem. You trust that business at that moment because they're solving a problem that you have. At that moment, because they are solving your problem, the business is at a pretty high level of credibility in the client-business relationship. Now, I have seen a number of programs and systems saying that after about a week you call clients up and ask them for a certain number of referrals. In this transaction model, they trusted you the most when they were making the purchase. If you haven't built the relationship further, then the best time to ask for referrals would have been when they were making the purchase.

I can't tell you how many times I have been asked for referrals when I really did not have a great relationship with that person or business. It seems that people are either one way or the other—either they don't ask for referrals or they ask for referrals too soon. The trick here is to build a strong enough relationship with your referral sources so that they want to help you. It is inherent in our human nature to want to help others, especially those with whom we have a relationship.

WRIGHT

I've heard that when forming a plan for anything, it's a good idea to focus on goals and return on investment, so how do these relate to a marketing plan?

MARTIN

That is another great question. It's true that whenever you're forming any kind of business goal or business plan you ensure that the plan has a way to measure the goal or effectiveness of the plan. Specifically, we are speaking about marketing plans here.

Now, I certainly advocate having a balanced marketing plan that includes advertising, word-of-mouth, as well as other marketing methods that may be applicable, which certainly includes PR (public relations). The important thing, as you have pointed out, is to ensure that this plan is working—that this plan is providing ROI (return on investment). The only way for you to know whether or not your plan is working is for you to have a way to measure it. You should be able to measure the effectiveness of each part of your plan.

As you're planning, you want to focus on setting goals for each aspect of marketing that you are employing. I recommend setting a number of incremental goals. Incremental goals let you measure your progression to a larger goal, and let you know if this part of the plan is working.

An example of a marketing goal specific to one part of a marketing plan would be something like wanting to grow your business by 10 percent by implementing a specific strategy.

I just talked to a friend of mine, who manages a staffing company. The company provides temporary and temp to perm staffing. She was telling me about implementing a new marketing strategy to the marketing plan four years ago. They had decided that the goal for this strategy was to get 5 percent of their total business from close contact networking. Now, this is exactly what I am talking about. My friend's business associates decided, before they executed a marketing strategy, what an acceptable return on their investment would be. (By the way, they get approximately 10 percent of their total business from that one activity now.) They were very specific; their goal was not to get 5 percent of their business from networking or word-of-mouth marketing. The goal was to get 5 percent of their business from a specific activity within the networking portion of their marketing plan. It is also important to note that from the beginning, they made sure to track the amount of business coming from that activity.

So many times I walk into businesses and I find out that they're doing many different types of marketing, usually without any plan or consistency that would tie these different activities together. In fact, in small businesses, this is more the norm. Small business owners tend to be so focused on what their product or service is that they forget to even put marketing in the plan. That is, until down the road at some point when they realize the need. I can't tell you the number of small businesses I have seen personally that have opened, have begun executing their plan, and then begin to worry about how they will get clients.

Another way that is all too common is that entrepreneurs will be running their business when an advertising sales rep comes to them with a great idea. Now, the entrepreneur has to figure out how to pay for the advertising that they need, many times because they did not budget for advertising or they are already spending their budget. Many times this happens because there is no marketing plan in place. Even if the entrepreneur wanted to cut back spending on less effective methods to divert money to this new idea, there is no measurement of effectiveness, and the entrepreneur doesn't know what is working and what isn't working. The result often is that the entrepreneur spends more money than planned and doesn't even know what marketing strategy is working and what marketing strategy is a waste of money, let alone what form of marketing is returning the best.

What I am saying is that the marketing plan is essential to business. Plan your marketing according to goals and measure your marketing so that you know what is working and what isn't working. With this knowledge, you can adjust your plan accordingly. It might not need to be said, but I want to really emphasize, *expect ROI from your marketing.* If you aren't getting an ROI from your marketing dollars, change your activities.

WRIGHT

What is the first step to forming a successful marketing plan for a business?

MARTIN

The first step for forming a successful marketing plan for a business is to figure out *who your customer will be or who your customer is.* That may seem very basic and too simplistic, but unless you know to whom you're selling, to whom you're communicating, and who your customer is supposed to be, you can't figure out how to reach them in the marketplace. You've got to know who needs your products or service—what market niche that might be. Believe me, there are a number of people who get into a business and they think that everybody can use what they have; that's never the case. It is more likely the case that your specific market is going to be a niche based on the type of people you relate to. Knowing what market niche you serve helps you form your marketing plan so that those are the customers you are reaching.

A story comes to mind that I think illustrates this point very well. A friend of mine was a mortgage professional. She was a widow of dentist. She realized that first-time homebuyers weren't her target market. She loved them and they were great people and clients, but she realized that she didn't enjoy working with them and she didn't communicate with them as well as she did with other clients.

She realized that her target market was the large loan market. The individuals who were looking for larger mortgages were customers with whom she could relate on a personal level. She could communicate with them better and the loans were more enjoyable to process. There were a number of mortgage professionals who wanted to do the same kinds of large loans at that time, but they didn't communicate with the clients as well, they didn't know what went into buying the larger house. She did, because that was the market she had come from. Knowing this helped her focus her marketing efforts on the niche that was best for her. She no longer spent time, effort, or money seeking first-time home buyers.

At the same time I had another friend who dealt in the B & C grade mortgage market. She had strong products and strong knowledge of this market.

Both individuals were mortgage professionals but they had totally different market segments, totally different groups of clients, and their groups of clients had different personalities, read different magazines, and thought differently. Even though both of these professionals operated in the same city, they were dealing with two distinct types of people. It was almost as though they were dealing with two distinct cultures, one foreign to the other. This is because they served two different market niches.

It's very important to be realistic about who your product or service is best marketed to or who your product or service is going to be bought by. Who is going to be the purchaser? Who is going to be the customer? Once you know the niche that you are going to serve or are currently serving, then design your marketing plan around the target market for your business. You may even refine the product or service you have while you are figuring this out, so that you can better serve this target market.

WRIGHT

So how much do you think it costs to form and perhaps implement an effective marketing plan?

MARTIN

David, I don't know that there is a simple answer to this question. I have worked with quite a few businesses and each has a different marketing budget. You can go from spending millions of dollars for national marketing plans to very cost effective, local marketing plans that are built much more on a "gorilla" marketing concept. It really depends on who you're trying to reach and somewhat on size.

I always like to suggest that you form your marking plan at the same time or as soon as you've got the product, unless you form a marketing plan first, and decide what product you will market to based on what is needed.

The market, your location in the country, and how you are going to reach into that market segment determines how much you're going to spend on marketing. It can be very expensive or you can do it on a shoestring, but I do recommend that you have a budget for it. Be certain that a portion of your budget for that first year is built around your marketing plan. Even shoestring marketers are spending money on marketing. This doesn't mean radio advertising—they're spending money for people to go out and put flyers on doors, to stand out along side of the road with a sign, and to do other things. Nobody is marketing for zero dollars, every marketing plan has a budget. Even when you get into word-of-mouth and relationship marketing, there is a time factor that goes into that. There is still an expense factor as well—a .

Soto sum up and answer your question in one simple phrase, the cost of a marketing plan varies but there will always be a cost. Be prepared to spend something to market your business.

WRIGHT

How complicated is an effective marketing plan? Is it out of most people's range?

MARTIN

I tend to be the kind of person who can complicate things quite a bit. It's interesting that the trainers with whom I work now are always reiterating something back to me, *Keep It Simple, Keep It Simple Stupid.* An effective marketing plan does not have to be extremely complicated. I'd say an effective marketing plan can be very simple.

Here again we're going back to the target market. Look at your target market and determine how you can reach into that niche. The cost is going to depend on the market you're trying to reach. If you're trying to reach twenty-year-old males, then whatever marketing you do should be focused as specifically as possible to twenty-year-old males. We should remember that they listen to different radio stations, they read different newspapers, they look at different Web sites, and they do different activities during the day. If you look at different market niches, you will find them participating in drastically different leisure activities. Knowing your target market is very important.

Once you know your target market, the next step is to determine the simplest way to get to them.

I discussed word-of-mouth marketing, so let's use some specific examples here—focusing on how simple a word-of-mouth marketing plan can be for a market niche. Let's look at a specific product or service. We'll say we're looking for people who will buy custom cabinets. I just happened to be working with custom cabinet maker this morning. When custom cabinet makers want to build a word-of-mouth marketing plan, they focus on people who want to buy custom cabinets. So, examining this market niche, we ask the questions, who buys custom cabinets and what do they look like? People who want to buy custom cabinets are typically home owners. They are either in the process of building a custom home or have an older home. They may have just purchased the older home or they may be looking at selling it. There is a lot of variance. They could be people who have been in the home for a while or they could be people who just moved into the home and want to change the look of their kitchen.

When formulating a word-of-mouth marketing plan, look for potential referral partners. These partners would be businesses that also sell in the same marketing niche but that do not compete with your business. What businesses sell to homeowners and don't compete with a custom cabinet maker? Other businesses that provide services to homeowners improving their homes would be interior designers, painters, heating and air people, and plumbers. Developing relationships with these potential referral partners would set the custom cabinet maker in a win-win-win situation.

A side effect of these relationships is that our cabinet maker now represents four or five businesses. He or she can offer more solutions to customers' needs than a custom cabinet maker who represents only himself or herself. The converse is also true. The four or five businesses also represent the cabinet maker. This represents a plan that's fairly simple—build a relationship with three or four people. Now that doesn't sound too complicated, does it David?

WRIGHT

Not hard at all.

MARTIN

You as the cabinet maker can build a relationship with three or four people who can represent you when they go into homes. Now, getting the right three or four people is where it might not be so easy, but it's certainly not complicated. The most effective word-of-mouth marketing plan is establishing relationships with five to eight referral partners—businesses or individuals who sell to your market niche but who do not compete with you.

WRIGHT

You mentioned relationships, and before that we spoke of investing in social capital. Will you explain social capital to our readers and specifically will you talk a little bit about the process for building relationships?

MARTIN

Yes, I have mentioned relationships a number of times, haven't I David? Relationships are key to building word-of-mouth marketing. Social capital is a newer concept that may not be fully understood by many. Social capital is a pretty big concept. Social capital is the glue that binds people together. It's also based on relationships but the concept relates to more than just the business market, it relates to all aspects of our life.

I once read an article by some social scientists about social capital in the "New South." The New South is defined as cities that have rapid growth and have a large influx of new residents. I was specifically interested in this article because I do a lot of work in Charlotte, North Carolina, and Charlotte is considered a New South city. This means that Charlotte has a lot of residents who are originally from elsewhere. The reason this article was so fascinating to me was that when people move to a new area or city, they start out with a whole lot less social capital. Social capital is the term that was coined to represent the strength of the social relationships a person has.

We understand business capital as money that has been invested with a business—the financial assets that a business has at its disposal. Social capital, like business capital, is based on the relationships we have invested in—relationships that can translate into social assistance. An example of social capital could be when you have someone you can call in an emergency to watch your children. Another example I have heard used to measure relationships is if you could ask to borrow someone's car.

So investing, social capital, relationships and investing in social capital, in a social sense, is about building emotional bank accounts. This is a concept that Stephen Covey talks about in his book, *The 7 Habits of Highly Effective People.* Building these social capital bank accounts is about investing your time into building relationships with others.

Dr. Misner, of the Referral Institute and BNI, has trademarked the VCP™ Process, a process that we use to explain how relationships are built. All relationships go through the same process. If you use a personal relationship as an example it may clarify things a little. Realizing that relationships are relationships, personal relationships go through the same process that business relationships go through. I, for one, had to learn this. I thought that business relationships were different. Unlike some though, I did a whole lot better on my business relationships than I did in some of my personal relationships. It was enlightening for me to learn the VCP Process. VCP stands for Visibility, Credibility, and then Profitability.

Essentially, using this process as a guide, we see that before you can ever build a relationship you have to see someone. You have to see people and know that they exist or you can't build a relationship with them. You get to know them and what you have in common and you build rapport with them. Now, just because you've built rapport doesn't mean that you have a very tight relationship, it just means that you've started the relationship.

After you have built rapport, have some commonality, know a person, and know what the person likes, the next step is to move yourself into "C" or credibility in the process. Credibility is that point where you begin to trust each other. I always like use personal relationships as examples. Many people are probably better at personal relationships. For example, think about the dating phase of a personal relationship, you become aware of a person, whether by seeing him or her or by hearing about the person. You decide that you would like to get to know the person better. After initially building some rapport, the next step is dating. When you date a person, you are building credibility—that's what's really happening. You're building rapport, true, but you're also building credibility—you're learning to trust each other.

Think about it, if a man shows up on time, it tells a woman quite a bit about him. How a woman dresses tells a man quite a bit about her and the relationship. Well, it's the same in a business relationship, except that in business what restaurants you like might not be quite as important. Business relationships are more related to trusting the way the other person does business. When you move into credibility you are beginning to trust each other.

WRIGHT

So how do relationships help you with your marketing plan?

MARTIN

That's a very well-timed question because we haven't gotten to the "P" in VCP yet. Relationships help you with your marketing plan when they move into the "P" phase of the process. We talked earlier about the eight different referral sources, one of which is customers. We talked about having referral partners and I mentioned that the goal is to have between five and eight referral partners. When you can get into the profitability phase of a business relationship with between five and eight referral partners who serve the same market niche as you do, but who do not compete with you, you will really begin to see the return on your investment. This will make a huge difference in your marketing plan.

The profitability phase of the VCP Process is a highly misunderstood phase. Many think that when a customer or client or associate makes a purchase from them that they have moved into the "P" phase. This is an incorrect assumption. The profitability that I am talking about is when two individuals are in a mutually beneficial relationship—one where referrals are passed on a regular, predictable basis.

Once you figure out the target market correctly you then build relationships with other individuals who serve the same target market. These relationships can serve as your communications conduit into your target market. Anytime you get a new client, he or she is potentially a client for your referral partners and vice versa. Profitable relationships go way beyond credibility. Profitable relationships are when your partner is willing to put his or her name on the line and tell others that they should do business with you. The same applies to your customers as well. A profitable relationship means that you are willing to recommend your referral partners to your customers.

If we apply this to your relationships with your best customers, we can see how profitability works. Think about these relationships. Your best customers are probably sending you more business regularly. Wouldn't you say that's correct, David?

WRIGHT

Absolutely.

MARTIN

So, when you get a good customer he or she refers you to someone else. Why might that be? Your best customers are referring you because they have bought from you enough times that they know you're never going to "drop the ball"—they know your credibility is beyond reproach. More than likely you have a personal or, on some level, a deeper than "just a customer walking in and buying a product" relationship with them. They feel indebted to you because you've helped them in their life or business, you've helped them and now they want to help you. They're sending you business.

Now, the greatest thing about this relationship marketing, or word-of-mouth marketing, or whatever name you call it is that you have set up what I have come to refer to as a win, win, win.

I want you to think back to a time when you've given a referral. When you give a referral, who wins? The person you gave the referral to wins because he or she gets more business, right? Now the customer had a problem, remember? You referred the customer to somebody that would solve his or her problem, so the customer won and he or she is happy, right?

WRIGHT

Absolutely.

MARTIN

So it's win-win; it's a two-way street. What about your relationship with the customer or the person you knew—the person you referred to get his or her problem solved? Does that person think more highly of you?

WRIGHT

The person should be thankful.

MARTIN

Yes, the person should be thankful. Believe me, if you referred somebody who has a problem, that person is very thankful when the problem is solved. You have just moved your relationship further through the process, and at the same time, you've helped and furthered your relationship with the person to whom you referred the business. Three people are winning in the process of the referral. In my mind, this is the only time you have this situation in business.

Many times there are people out there negotiating win-lose—"I'm going to get the money out of this customer's pocket." If you're in referral marketing, it's about building relationships with your customers, your clients, and everybody else, including your vendors, your sources, and referral partners. You're building relationships with them, you're making sure everyone is winning, and everyone's boat is going to rise when that tide is coming in; everyone becomes happy. I like to think it's the best way to do business period because of establishing a win-win-win relationship out there.

WRIGHT

So a couple of times you've mentioned keeping things simple. Would you give our readers some examples of simplifying to make a marketing plan more effective?

MARTIN

I certainly can. Many people end up making their marketing plans very complicated. As I said earlier, they don't have to be complicated, they should actually be kept simple. As my staff tells me, keep it simple Rich. In fact, they should be very simple. Use the measurements and cut what isn't getting a good return on investment.

Let's think about a typical marketing plan for a moment. Let's assume that you have word-of-mouth, a couple of radio spots running on multiple stations, and you're doing some print advertising. You look at two or three of the radio stations that you're advertising on and they're getting a nice return, but they may not be getting you the return on investment that the one other radio station is. Simplify. Your target market is responding to that one radio station and you're going to get a better return on investment by increasing your spots on that one station as you reallocate the money you are already using. It may even be that you can save money in this process, while still increasing your market share. It is important to note that you have to have that measurement in place before you can evaluate your plan.

Now, radio advertising people and anybody who is selling advertising or marketing out there may not want to hear this, but if you're getting a better return on investment through certain forms of marketing, then you're going to make more money if you drop the ones that you're not getting a return on and spend more on the ones where you are getting the return. It is that simple.

WRIGHT

So what are the steps that people can take, starting, say, tomorrow to improve their marketing?

MARTIN

I think there are about five steps people should take to improve their marketing; and any business can stand to improve its marketing.

Step one is to refine and define your target market. Refine and define your target market as to who they are and then learn everything you can about them. I like to say, find out what they look like, smell like, find out where they hang out, and find out anything you can about that target market. The more you know about your target market, the more you know how to reach your customers in the communication process. The more you know how they think, the more you know what your marketing should look and sound like. You need to know what they value, and reach out to them. Communicate about topics that they value, communicate the way they think, and get the communication to where they're going to hear it. Step one is find out more about your target market, or refine your target market, the narrower or more precise you definition your target market, the easier and simpler it is for you to communicate with them. Many people think you have to have a broad spectrum of advertising and marketing to reach as many people as possible, I disagree. My advice is to focus on your target market and then communicate specifically with them.

The second step is to look at your business. Analyze your business and figure out what is unique about it, especially what's unique about your business as it relates to your target market. What is specifically unique and special about your business will be something that you want to communicate to your target market. It's the reason why your target market is coming to you and it's a reason why they're identifying with your product and why it speaks to them. Figure out what that uniqueness is. It could be called a USP (Unique Selling Proposition). We like to call it a UBP (Unique Buying Proposition).

Number three is to look at all the marketing you're currently doing. If you're currently in business or if you've just started a business, either way, make sure all your marketing and marketing materials have the same message. This doesn't mean that all of the materials have to say the same thing, but make sure there is integrity in the message that you are conveying to your target market. This message should speak to your target market and should speak to the uniqueness of your business. You do you see how this all comes back to that target market and then builds upon it, right, David?

Oh, by the way, if you should have a business that serves multiple target markets, the answer is simple. Each division of your business deserves its own marketing plan to reach the distinct target markets rather than trying to jumble the plans together.

Okay, so we've got the target market, we've got what's unique about your business, and then we have unifying or bringing everything into concert as far as your marketing materials.

This final bit also includes the messages that people are using when they answer the phones, the hold messages on your telephone, the flyers you distribute, even messages on your invoices. Everything—every piece of paper, every time you touch a customer, every time you touch anyone—should communicate to your target market and should point to the uniqueness of your business.

After you're done with the third step, then I would say implement a word-of-mouth marketing program by determining who your potential referral partners are. This fourth step is to figure out who else serves your target market that doesn't compete with you. Figure out who these potential referral sources are and put those names into a list as soon as you can. This list doesn't have to be restricted to names, it could also be simply job positions or job titles or company titles that serve your same target market.

After you've got this list, the fifth step is to get out of your cave and start building relationships—relationships that are really key to building your business are those with potential referral partners. Build these relationships, build them strong, and build them deep. Look for six good, solid relationships with people who serve your target market and build the relationships deep so that these partners are talking to every one of their customers about you. Of course you are talking to every one of your customers about them as well. You start to service customers together. You are building a strong relationship—a strategic alliance that we call a profitable business relationship.

So there are just five steps. None of them, I would like to point out, are extremely difficult, but at the same time (as Dr. Misner likes to say), it's not rocket science, however, it certainly isn't always easy to do. It takes concentration, it takes effort, and it takes focus to build this marketing plan and to go out and start building those relationships in the marketing world.

WRIGHT

Well, Richard, I really do appreciate all this time you've taken with me this afternoon to answer these questions. This is fascinating information; it almost seems so simple that I might be able to do it!

MARTIN

Everyone can do it, David. I've seen a number of different people who thought it was complicated. But as I said, once we break it down to the keep-it-simple stage, it doesn't have to be difficult. So you're right, everyone can do it.

WRIGHT

Well, I really do appreciate your taking this time with me. I have learned a lot and I'm sure our readers will.

MARTIN

Thanks, I certainly have enjoyed our time.

WRIGHT

Today we've been talking with Richard Martin who is the Chief Catalyst of International Business Fuel. He works with entrepreneurs, business owners, sales teams, and professionals creating entrepreneurial success. As an entrepreneurial leadership expert specializing in business growth, Rich helps business people connect with their passion and people to generate profits. You've probably come to the same conclusion that I have—he knows what he's talking about.

Richard, thank you so much being with us today on *GPS for Success*.

About the Author

Richard Martin is the Chief Catalyst of International Business Fuel. He began his career in the United States Army where he was an honor graduate from both the Army Ranger School and the Special Forces Qualifications Course. Now he works with entrepreneurs, business owners, sales teams, and professionals creating entrepreneurial success. As an entrepreneurial leadership expert specializing in business growth, Rich helps business people connect with their passion and people to generate profits. He is the developer of the Business Propellant training program and the Catalyst Groups concept. His fast-paced, results-driven seminars have built him the reputation as a trainer who maximizes what everyone takes away.

Richard Martin
4994 Lower Roswell Rd.
Marietta, GA 30068
678.576.0113
rich@intlbizfuel.com
www.intlbizfuel.com

CHAPTER SIX

The Heart of Success:

10 Proven Strategies that Build Networking, Confidence, and Effectiveness

An interview with...

Dawn Billings

DAVID WRIGHT (WRIGHT)

Today we're talking with Dawn Billings, CEO and founder of the Heartlink Women's Network, an innovative international networking and marketing organization that launched its first location in Sedona, Arizona, in May of 2008, and since then has grown to more than one hundred and forty-five locations in the United States, Canada, and Australia. Dawn also founded the HeartAlliance.com, an online professional women's networking community that links women around the world, and TROVA Women Business Directory especially to showcase, advertise, and support small business owners. Dawn is also the creator of a new parenting tool called Capables™ (*GetCapables.com*), which is touted to revolutionize parenting around the world. She has a passion for making a difference in the lives of women and children and travels nationally as a parenting and relationship expert. Dawn is a highly sought-after speaker and trainer who specializes in entitlement issues that are currently plaguing our society.

Dawn has a master's degree in Clinical Psychology, while her doctorate studies focus on organizational psychology and personality. She is also the author of over twenty books. Dawn is also the President of Dawn L. Billings, Inc. a training and executive coaching company where she is a consultant to executives and organizations focusing on teamwork, communication skills, improving productivity, and retaining top talent. Dawn is the creator and author of an amazingly simple but powerful assessment tool known as the "Primary Colors Personality Test." Dawn's personality test was administered to over sixty thousand couples and families in 2007 and even more than that in 2008. The test helps couples communicate better with each other and with their children.

Dawn, welcome to *GPS for Success: Goals and Proven Strategies,* and I have to tell you I'm exhausted just reading your bio.

DAWN BILLINGS (BILLINGS)

I know; I was exhausted listening.

WRIGHT

So it seems that among your many accomplishments you've taken the art of professional networking to the next level. You've created two wonderful marketing and networking tools designed especially to help female entrepreneurs explode their businesses. I understand that you also have a real passion for linking women to wonderful resources, new ideas, products and services, and especially the hearts of one another. Because of your lifelong commitments to benefit women and children, in 2008 you were chosen as one of fifteen women of achievement by the Cobb County Georgia YWCA. More notably, you were selected as one of the nation's eighty emerging women leaders from three thousand two hundred applicants by *Oprah* magazine and the White House Project for your socially dynamic programs that benefit women and children.

Will you tell our readers a bit about your mission to help women and children and how you got started?

BILLINGS

Yes. I've always had an enormous desire to help women and children. I think that children are the future of the world and if you support, encourage, and inspire women, then they will definitely take care of, support, nurture, encourage, and inspire children. Doing all I can to help bless women and their success makes this wonderful big circle that benefits the entire world.

I learned early in life that one kindness, one gift, one stand-tall action can touch a heart and change the direction of a life, and can even create a better world. When I was a young girl, we were very, very poor. We didn't have indoor plumbing, we had no hot water in the house, and we had very little clothing. Therefore, I did not have as many choices about what I was going to wear to school and I was very embarrassed by this.

I had a second grade teacher who was kind to me. I guess she took an interest in me because I was bright. On the first day of school for second grade there was a flyer on my desk about joining Brownies. I was so excited; I knew about Brownies because my cousin had a friend who got to be one and I knew they wore uniforms. I was excited because I believed that if I had a uniform I could finally be like everyone else and fit in.

I ran home after school with that flyer and couldn't wait to hand it to my mom. She sat down and cried because we did not have money for the uniform and dues. My father told me it would take a miracle for me to become a Brownie. My mother whispered that miracles were real and although we were poor, hope was the poor man's bread and it was my job to eat up.

The next day our teacher gave us an assignment. She asked us to write about our favorite color. My friends picked bright colors like green, blue, red, and purple. I picked brown. I wrote that brown was the color of the soil where food grew, and brown was the color of tree trunks that held up the fruit. Brown was the color of the uniform of the most wonderful organization in the world—the Brownies—but I wasn't going to get to be one because we didn't have any money.

My teacher called me into her office a couple of weeks later and there was a box on her desk. She asked me to look inside the box. When I did, there was a Brownie uniform. She kept apologizing that the uniform was not new. She said it had belonged to her sister's daughter who was a year older than I was. She had asked her sister to send me her niece's old uniform. I didn't care that the uniform was old or used. I just wanted it to fit. It did!

My teacher knew that I had a dream to be something special. She did all she could to help be a part of something that made a difference and that was bigger than I was. She knew that I had an incredible passion to be a Brownie because if I had a uniform, nobody would know that I didn't have many clothes—I would be like everyone else.

When she gave me the uniform, she told me she was going to pay my dues for the year. I asked what I could do to pay her back and she said, "Become Great." She told me that greatness is never an accident, it's always a choice. What she wanted from me was to choose to be great. She told me she wanted me to inspire others to choose to be great and to be the kind of leader she knew I had the talent to be. That just stuck in my heart and every day since then I hear her words. I have committed my life to doing what she asked.

I wrote this story in my very first book, *Greatness in Children: Learn the Rules*. Jack Canfield and Mark Victor-Hansen, authors of the *Chicken Soup for the Soul* series, read it and called me and asked if they could publish the story in their *Chicken Soup for the Christian Families Soul* book. I couldn't remember my teacher's name, although I heard her voice in my heart every day and she had completely transformed my life. If they were going to put the story in one of the *Chicken Soup for the Soul* books, I had to track her down and use her real name. I found her. It was forty years later (I was forty-seven years old). I learned that my second grade class was her first class, and when I found her forty years later, she was teaching her last year. I was able to honor and thank her and put her real name in the Chicken Soup book.

I invited her husband to bring her to where I was speaking. She didn't know what was happening. When I told the story in front of hundreds of people and honored her with flowers, it was very moving. Her family was crying—everyone in the audience was crying. She had never realized what an influence she had been in my life. No student had ever come back to her and thanked her in such a public way.

It really taught me that you do not know how a kindness, a connection, a conversation can affect the lives of others. Often it is the small gifts like believing in someone or inspiring or encouraging the dreams in the heart of another that can make an enormous difference. Because of my teacher, I have spent my entire life touching thousands of women and children's lives.

One kindness and one encouraging act made a huge difference. Now my dream is to touch enough women around the world so they'll go out and touch everyone they know, who will go out and touch everyone they know, until we transform the entire planet. That is what The Heart Link Network is really all about.

WRIGHT

What a great goal. So let's talk specifically about The Heart Link Network® and the Heart Alliance™. There are thousands of networking organizations that exist. Why did you feel it was necessary to create The Heart Link Network and your online professional community, The HeartAlliance.com? How is The Heart Link Network different from other networking organizations and what makes it so unique?

BILLINGS

You are correct—there are thousands of networking organizations that exist, but most of them are not built specifically for women and designed around the female endocrine system like The Heart Link Network. When I really started researching how best to help women live their dreams and succeed in business, I realized that if they're not connected heart-to-heart, then they don't have the internal or external resources to really succeed.

As I began my research on networking models, I realized that 99 percent of all networking models were built on a male model of networking, which made sense because the male model of networking, marketing, and advertising has been the dominant model for the last fifty or sixty years. The male model of networking and marketing is called *interruption marketing*. Interruption marketing was created when the radio was invented. Marketing and advertising experts realized that if you can capture people's attention and then interrupt it with ads, you could sell to complete strangers. This was revolutionary and turned the marketing, advertising, and business world upside down. This model continued to pick up steam with the invention of the television, magazine ads, billboards, newspapers, etc. The interruption-marketing model changed the entire world of advertising and marketing.

The problem with interruption marketing is that, as it continued to grow, we were interrupted everywhere. We were being called at home and we ended up with do not call lists. People would walk up to you at a grocery store or outside of a restaurant and you would be interrupted there. Your television programs would be interrupted. Then TiVo and DVR were invented so that we could record shows and fast-forward through the interruptions. People got to the point where they just simply did not want to be interrupted anymore. When the Internet came we gave interruption a name—SPAM. We were more than tired of being interrupted.

If interruption marketing was declining in its effectiveness and certainly was not working in the same powerful unique way that it had when it first began, what should be done next? I saw people were tired of being bombarded and yet, there were so many women out there in various businesses who wanted to share the wonderful products and services they had to offer. The questions were what to do, and how to do it.

The problem I faced in finding an answer for this was that if people are tired of being interrupted and they're tired of being bombarded, how in the world were women supposed to let one another know about their products, services, and resources? If you can't interrupt people, how do you meet them? How do you create relationships with them? How do you serve them?

Traditional networking is built on interruption. You walk into a room where people are talking. You walk up and interrupt that conversation to introduce yourself. Interruption is something that makes women feel uncomfortable because we are built differently—our endocrine systems are different. I wanted to create a networking and marketing organization that was built totally on the female endocrine system. It would no longer be built on the interruption marketing model, but would be built on *permission marketing*.

When we were a more agricultural society, everything was based on permission marketing. For example, in a small town there were one or more people who owned the corner store. These folks knew everyone in the town. They knew who quilted, who grew corn or raised cows. When they would stock the shelves in the general store, they purchased items that might benefit their customers. Their customers were happy to be contacted because they were also friends—they had *permission* to share information with their friends.

When I created The Heart Link Network (*TheHeartLinkNetwork.com*), I added the women's online social community, The Heart Alliance (*TheHeartAlliance.com*). I created it based on building relationships with people who want to meet other women and learn from each other. Everyone who attends our meetings wants to know what others have to offer and how these products/services might benefit their lives. They also want to develop relationships that can last a lifetime. That's what makes The Heart Link Network vastly different and very unique from other networking models.

I also wanted to develop a model that was inclusive of professional women who have traditionally been excluded from networking. These include teachers, nurses, and especially the most important profession—mothers. I didn't want a *business* networking model; what I really wanted to create was a *professional* networking model that was inclusive of professional women and stay-at-home moms.

I was tired of going to meetings where women would stand up and say, "Well, I'm *just a mom*." I believe that being a mother is one of the most honorable, necessary, and challenging professions that exists in the world. I created The Heart Link Network so that every month we are excited to honor a different segment of women in our society who are traditionally overlooked. When they come to our networking meetings, we as businesswomen stand up and thank them and honor them for going into the profession of teaching or nursing or deciding to stay at home and focus on raising children.

It's very unique in today's world for business professionals to do this because nobody is taking time to honor these women. It gives all of the women an opportunity to get to know one another, to create relationships with one another, and, more importantly, to rebuild community with one another. When women are in community with one another, and have relationships with one another, the entire community benefits by becoming stronger.

WRIGHT

You launched The Heart Link Network in May 2008 and had over a hundred locations in your first one hundred and twenty days. That's an amazing feat. So what do you believe caused such an explosion of growth across the United States, Canada, and the company you just launched in Australia? How did you do it?

BILLINGS

I didn't do it. This company and its mission were completely blessed by God. The women who have joined me in this mission to love, encourage, and inspire women humble me every day. They are the most amazing loving spirits. They are basically a volunteer army of extraordinary and giving women who love other women and want to help them succeed.

The beautiful thing is I had a dream—it was a dream that has resonated with so many other women and they shared it with other women who shared it with other women. There has been a marvelous ripple effect of giving, caring, sharing, and empowering women. The entire company has totally been built on word-of-mouth, integrity, and experience. Because of word-of-mouth sharing, in our first year we launched over a one hundred and twenty locations in three countries. That's unheard of in the marketplace today. It was done completely by women sharing with other women what we're all about and what we're doing. We anticipate that our growth is going to be steady. The economy has been hit very hard and families are suffering. One of the things we know is that when times are tough, we need relationships to support us even more. We will not stop until we see women being able to attend The Heart Link Network in every city in our nation.

We are dedicated to continuing to provide women with the resources, the connections, and the links that we think they need in order to live the greatest dreams in their hearts. The Heart Link Network has been working like magic—it's just fantastic and we can't wait until we are blessing a hundred thousand women around the world.

WRIGHT

You're considered one of today's top networking experts. What would you say are the top ten steps to networking with more effectiveness and confidence?

BILLINGS

Great question. I always like things broken down into easy steps, so I've listed them below:

1. You must have the heart of a giver.

The first thing is that you really have to network with a heart for blessing and benefiting the life of another. People can sense your heart. What's most wonderful is that once a woman discovers that the greatest networkers really are the greatest givers, then they realize how easy it is and they begin to love and enjoy networking.

Networking is really all about net-sharing, net-caring, and net-daring. That is why it is important to network until you feel comfortable and confident. The whole key to our model is that we really care about one another. Our company is built on what we call the Four Wins—we don't believe in just a simple win-win, which is wonderful, where you win and I win, but we believe it takes more than that. You need to win, I need to win, and then everyone we encounter in the community or our world needs to win; and God needs to win. If you can do any endeavor and meet these four criteria, we believe that you cannot fail because what you are doing is wonderful, good, and necessary.

We also believe that if you go into a networking environment and what you're focusing on is getting to know other people and creating relationships and trying to learn and understand exactly what others are doing and what they need, what will happen is that in turn people will begin to trust you and believe in you. They'll want to give back, help you, and do business with you. We all want to do business with people we know and like.

2. Make a decision that you are actually going to network.

The second important step in networking can be broken in two parts. The first part is *to decide that you're actually going to network.* Women need to make a conscious decision and a real commitment to actually becoming a master networker.

In order to be a master networker, you've got to show up. Showing up is always the first step to be great at anything, but especially when you're networking. All marketing is about consistency. You must be consistent and never give up. We must learn the power of the word *next.* After any disappointment, when we open our heart and mind to the possibility of what's *next,* it eases the pain of the disappointment. Some people I've known have attended a networking event, and if they didn't get immediate business, they wanted to give up. That's nonsense. In the marketing industry, each time you meet or encounter someone, it's called an *opportunity touch.* So every single time that you show up or meet someone, you're actually touching the person's life in some way. If you think about when you show up or have a conversation with someone that you are touching their life in some way, you'll do it differently than just having a conversation. It will actually cause something to occur in your heart where you really do feel like you're touching and enhancing the life of someone.

I just love that word "touch" because touch is what our two networking organizations The Heart Link Network and The Heart Alliance are all about. Networking is not about immediate business, it's about building relationships. If you have a disappointing conversation or something doesn't turn out exactly the way you want, then just tell yourself, "Okay, *next,*" and go on to the next person you can touch. Change your Networking into *next*working.

When you *next*work instead of network, you will discover that the second part of networking is to network with confidence. People can feel your confidence. They are inspired and encouraged by it. With each networking experience, a woman gains more confidence because she gains more knowledge, not only about products and services, but about herself and others. I think we're all afraid of what we don't understand. Knowledge can ease the effect of how others experience us in a networking environment. So if we make a conscious decision to network and do it with confidence, it will make all the difference.

3. Be interesting and interested.

We have a responsibility to be interesting when someone is listening to us, but even a bigger responsibility to be interested in what somebody else is saying.

I think it would be a good idea if every woman sat down and thought about writing a commercial describing herself. If you attempt this exercise and you have nothing to write about, well, I think that maybe it's time to figure out how to do something more interesting so that you would have something to write about. It's not just about networking; it's about sharing the life you're living. How can we possibly expect to be interesting to anyone else if we don't even interest ourselves? So I think it's important to just become interesting and then work on and strengthen your ability to be interested.

We learn a lot by just listening. We learn a lot by asking questions and trying to figure out who this person is and who do you know that can help this person, and who do I know that this person can help. It's a wonderful reciprocal circle. So find women that you think are worthy of "commercials" and then learn all about them. Then do all you can to make yourself worthy of a great commercial. I don't think you'll ever have any trouble being interesting when you're networking.

4. Take good care of yourself.

Too many women are so busy taking care of their families and friends and maybe their other responsibilities, whether it's volunteer work or church work that they don't have time (or they don't think they have time) to take care of themselves.

Networking with other women allows us to meet other great women. When we meet them, it gives us an opportunity to become friends with them. When we become friends with them, we develop support systems in our lives. We also learn all about these amazing new products and services, health and wellness ideas, beauty, education—all of these things that can help us take better care of ourselves. There is only one you and so the better you feel, the better you take care of yourself, and the better you take time for yourself, the more energy you'll actually have for your business, your family, or to help others.

5. Choose your relationships wisely.

This step is important, not just in networking, but in life. Networking is a wonderful way to meet a wide range of people and develop new friendships. While you're networking, find women you absolutely fall in love with as friends. Find women who have integrity and who are willing to support, encourage, and inspire you, but who will also love you enough to tell you the truth even if you might not respond well to it. I mean, that's what real friends are all about. It's the quality of relationship that makes us more of who we need to be when we develop friends we trust enough, who can really be honest with us, and who can help us see our "blind spots." We need to use our networking opportunities to build a community of at least five people in our lives with whom we feel safe, whom we trust enough to hold us accountable, and whom we feel we're mutually supported by. If you receive nothing from networking but that, then you will have absolutely become rich simply by networking.

6. Become a woman of integrity.

This step is vital. Not only find and befriend women of integrity, but actually live a life of integrity. Set high standards for the way you treat yourself and others and then live by those standards. Keep your word—keep your promises. Tell the truth and you'll be amazed at how people respect you, respond to you, and refer to you. Living in integrity means saying what you mean and meaning what you say. You follow through and do everything you say you're going to do. People can count on you, trust you, and believe in you.

7. Follow up and follow through.

Wow, I cannot stress how important this step is. Although this is certainly a part of the sixth step above—living our lives in integrity—I think it's so important that it actually deserves a number of its own. In order to be a successful networker or really successful at anything, you must follow up and follow through. Many people will tell you that success is in the follow-up. Listen to them; it's absolutely true. The person who follows up, takes building relationships seriously, and then follows through on what he or she promises is the one who will always reap the greatest rewards, not only in networking, but also in life.

8. Know yourself.

Don't network blind. Take time to really reflect on who you are. What are your strengths? What are you weaknesses? What are your gifts and talents? What have you got to give and what do you need to receive? Once you know the answer to these questions, it's easier to concentrate on your strengths and develop and strengthen your weaknesses. We are all different; we all have different talents and abilities. If you know and understand yours, you'll not only be better at serving others with them, but you'll be much better at recognizing women who have strengths that might help you be more successful as well.

Networking is all about collaboration and it's all about trust. If you would like to understand how to be the best networker you can be, start with understanding yourself and helping yourself be the best person and the best businessperson you can possibly be. If you'd like to understand yourself a little bit better, get a clear idea of what kind of personality or traits that you have.

One easy way to do this is to visit my Web site, *DawnBillings.com*. The Primary Colors Personality Test is right there. You can take it online and find out a lot more about your personality. There are millions of other personality inventories that you can also take if you want to broaden and deepen your understanding of yourself. Spend time in self-reflection. Journal. Then go back and read your thoughts and look at yourself from different angles. Understand what motivates you. What are your needs, greatest desires, greatest dreams, and fears? The more you know yourself, the more you can network more powerfully and effectively.

9. Don't be afraid of failure.

Fear offers nothing of any value to your life, it only stops you from living your dream and contributing the best you can be to the world. When you're afraid to do something because you're afraid you might fail, support yourself and do it anyway. Push past the fear; there is no success without failure. In fact, I love failure because indicates that I've risked something that I wasn't sure of—I tried it and I learned something. Now I can stand up and do it again and do it more wisely.

So think of failure as an ally to your success because it's through your failures that you'll learn your greatest lessons and develop your greatest strengths. If you fall down, fall over, fall away, or simply fall asleep, wake yourself up, dust yourself off, and move forward. Celebrate your failures; each one brings you one step closer to success.

10. Always give your best.

If you want the best for yourself, give the best of what you have to others. As said at the beginning of this list, networking is about giving. The more you give to others and the more you help others succeed, the more others will be inspired to help you.

There is a universal spiritual law that says what you give out comes back to you multiplied. That law is true. If people truly understood the truth of that law, we would hurry to give each other things. Giving is one of the most selfish things that we can do. If we understand that everything we give is multiplied and given back to us, then we realize that everything we give benefits ourselves—multiplied. So when you give the very best of yourself, the very best of the world will be given back to you. We can't out-give the giver.

When you attempt to help others achieve their dreams, you're actually ensuring that your dreams become reality.

In summary, if you show up with a giving heart, be there to help someone else, give your best, learn from the best, be your best, do your best, and expect the best, you will look in the mirror and see the reflection of a woman who networks and lives her life with great confidence. You'll experience the success that goes along with that.

WRIGHT

So how much does it cost to be a member of The Heart Link Network?

BILLINGS

One of the most wonderful things about The Heart Link Network is that it is one of the least expensive networking opportunities available. At The Heart Link Network, we provide a powerful way to network. Those who attend have three minutes to showcase their business. We provide a light dinner and complete attendance flexibility. And it only costs twenty dollars to attend. It's too good a deal to pass up. We believe we are the least expensive, most powerful, most effective networking tool that exists.

WRIGHT

So how do women find a location to attend?

BILLINGS

Oh that's easy; they go to our Web site, *theHeartLinkNetwork.com*, and they click on the locations button. There they'll see a map that has the United States, Canada, and Australia. They can click on their state and all of the cities that have locations in their state will pop up with contact information. If they click on that location it will take them directly to that Area Coordinator's page. You can pay your attendance fee with PayPal or give the area coordinator in your area a phone call and say, "I'd like to attend and get more information." It's really easy to find a location.

Any woman who would like to meet extraordinary women, expand her circle of influence, and increase her social capital should definitely attend The Heart Link Network gatherings.

WRIGHT

And if there is no location in the client's area?

BILLINGS

That's actually good news. If there is no location in your area it may mean that there is an opportunity for you to become the standout leader in your community. Our Heart Link Network leaders get an all-access pass to success with The Heart Link Network. It's the most extraordinary tool that can help any woman grow her business.

We teach our leaders the fine art of networking. We teach them how to go out and meet people, make new friends, and become widely known. We teach them how to bring women in the community together and bless them. Our Heart Link leaders become well-known and loved in their communities. Their businesses thrive because of their amazing giving hearts. So if there isn't a location near you it may be the best thing that ever happened to you. Find out how to create a location by filling out an application for more information.

WRIGHT

So tell me, what is *TheHeartAlliance.com* and what does it have to do with The Heart Link Network?

BILLINGS

The Heart Alliance is our online professional community for women. Women from all around the world are a part of it. It's a great place to meet and befriend like-minded women. It's a wonderful place and offers so many gifts to women everywhere.

We have created many gifts that we give to women who become a part of The Heart Alliance. One of the gifts we have created is the Heart-Notes dot com Garden (Heart-Notes.com). This is where women can discover beautiful heart-shaped flowers. They can pick their color and shape, insert a note of appreciation or thoughtfulness, and send it electronically to someone they love. It doesn't cost anything and it's just a wonderful way to say I'm thinking of you, I love you, I believe in you, I'm here for you.

The Heart Alliance women's online social networking community is really fun. Social networking communities are very popular, especially among women now. The world is smaller than ever because we can communicate around the world with a click of a button. We can all get to one another easily, so we can make friends in Ireland, Spain, Canada, or New Zealand. That's what The Heart Alliance allows us to do. It is now so easy to meet one another and create relationships electronically with people who are thousands of miles away.

We also have a gift called the *God Can* (*TheHeartAlliance.com/page/GodCan*). We know that in very stressful times, women need a place to vent their fears and frustrations. I spent fifteen years in private practice and I used to work with women who were really struggling with fears or anxieties. They had a memory they couldn't let go of or anger they couldn't release, so I created symbolic ways for them to release what was bothering them.

One of my favorites was to use a helium tank and fill up balloons. I had them write their fear or whatever they wanted to let go of on the balloon and just release it. They could watch it go up and away. Symbolically it was a very powerful experience.

I wanted to create a similar experience electronically where people could just let go of things or say prayers of appreciation, but primarily to let go of anxiety or fear. So I created the *God Can*. When you go to the God Can Web page, there is a little tablet that comes up. You type your fear or your anxiety on it. You then push a button that says, *I am done with this*. The note folds up and begins to float upward. The lid on the God Can rises, and the note floats into the God Can. When the lid closes, words come up to remind them, "Anytime you feel you can't, remember God can." It's non-denominational, beautiful, easy, and a beautiful experience. We've had women send us thank you letters from all around the world for creating this wonderful experience for them. Women consistently tell us what a wonderful resource and gift it is to help them eliminate their fears and their anxiety.

WRIGHT

So does it cost anything for women to become members of *TheHeartAlliance.com*?

BILLINGS

Not a penny. The basic membership in The Heart Alliance is free. It's The Heart Link Network's gift to women around the world. It's a vehicle to allow them connect, bond, grow, and prosper. I created The Heart Link Network as a much more high touch opportunity for women. We get to see each other, hug each other, come together, and meet with one another every month. I knew that a high touch experience was important, but I also realized that we needed to address the high tech needs of women in today's society. So I created The Heart Alliance as our high tech side for women to touch one another and The Heart Link Network as our high touch piece. These Internet sites work in tandem to help women to create and build relationships and communities around the world.

WRIGHT

So women can go to www.HeartAlliance.com today and simply sign up or sign in using their name and e-mail address to experience this delightful God Can of yours.

BILLINGS

Absolutely. They can experience it and then I hope they share it with everyone they think would be blessed by it. It doesn't cost anybody anything, but gives so much comfort to their heart.

WRIGHT

I understand that although you're known internationally as the architect of The Heart Link Network and www.TheHeartAlliance.com, and TROVA Women Business Directory, plus you've authored more than twenty books on various relationships, parenting, success, entitlement, and networking topics, your favorite accomplishment is something very unique. That unique creation is a parenting tool that is also a wonderful toy for children and has been praised by parenting experts who say it can revolutionize parenting around the world. Am I getting that right?

BILLINGS

Yes. It is my heart's delight and it is brand new. These wonderful toys for children and great tools for parents are called Capables. Everyone who has seen them—parenting experts, teachers, counselors, ministers—is so excited about them because they are very, very special. My Capables team and I couldn't be more excited. Our first five hundred Capables will be given to military families who have one spouse deployed because the parents who are left are in a very difficult situation. They have a spouse who is gone and they are concerned greatly about their welfare and their health. They're 24/7 parents with no relief, and they're all by themselves. Since they give so much and serve us so much, I wanted to give back to those families. I will also be giving all of the training, the books, and everything that goes with them to military families. Once they've had the training and are using the Capables then we're going to bring in some researchers to evaluate the program. We will then find others who want to help me get the money together for more military families. We're very, very excited about using Capables in that way. They're just wonderful. They truly do take the work out of parenting and turn it into play.

WRIGHT

Is this the first parenting and child learning system of its kind ever created?

BILLINGS

Yes. Actually, no one has ever created a plush toy to be utilized in this way. It teaches children to be extraordinary; and it teaches them things like foresight and planning, delayed gratification, self-control, emotional intelligence, and more. This is the culmination of thirty-five years of gathering knowledge and data. I spent four years in its design and development.

The reason I created the Capables is because new parents are on their own. Children don't come with an ownership manual; you give birth and basically there you are. There are many parenting books, but there has never been a parenting toy or tool that teaches parents how to parent powerfully and effectively while simultaneously helping children to become extraordinary successful people in the process. And it's fun. I wanted to help parents around the world. Parenting is the most awesome important job that people can have. I wanted to make it easy, I wanted to make it effective, but most of all, I wanted to make it fun and less stressful.

We all have great dreams for our children and the Capables help our children to grow into extraordinary people who have compassion and who care about others in their world. Capables help children learn to be people who can set goals and keep them, who know how to have a great dream and nurture it in their hearts, who know how to be generous, give back to their society, who know how to stand tall for their values, and who have great character. All of this can be taught with this simple, little, beautiful plush animal. So this new parenting toy has caused quite a stir around the world.

WRIGHT

Well, what a great conversation. This is amazing. I think the next time I read the dictionary, your picture might be next to the word "creativity." It seems like you've got a lot of things going. I'm not sure how you keep all the balls in the air.

I really appreciate all the time you've taken to answer these questions. I have learned a lot here. I took copious notes on your ten important steps to successful networking, starting at be someone who wants to help, all the way down to always give your best, and I'm going to try to live by that. That's good information regardless of whether or not you apply it to networking; I guess you realize that. I really think our readers are going to get a great amount of information and inspiration from this chapter.

BILLINGS

Thank you so much. This interview was a pleasure and I love helping in any way I can.

WRIGHT

Today we've been talking with Dawn Billings, the CEO and Founder of The Heart Link Women's Network, (www.TheHeartLinkNetwork.com), a women's networking and marketing organization with more than one hundred and forty-five locations in the United States, Canada, and Australia. She also founded www.TheHeartAlliance.com, an online professional women's networking community that links women all around the world, and TROVA Women Business Directory, an online directory for women who own small businesses. If that weren't enough she is also the President of Dawn L. Billings, Inc., a training and executive coaching company and she is creator of the new and amazing parenting tool called the Capables (www.GetCapables.com).

Dawn, thank you so much for being with us today on *GPS for Success: Goals and Proven Strategies.*

BILLINGS

Thank you.

About the Author

Dawn Billings is CEO and founder of The Heartlink Women's Network, an innovative international networking and marketing organization. The HLN launched its first location in Sedona, Arizona, in May of 2008 and now has more than one hundred and forty-five locations in the United States, Canada, and Australia. Dawn also founded the HeartAlliance.com, an online professional women's networking community that links women around the world, and TROVA™ Women Business Directory (www.TROVAWomenBusinessDirectory.com), an online business directory that advertises, showcases, and supports women-owned businesses. Dawn is also the creator of a new parenting tool called Capables™ (www.GetCapables.com), which is touted to revolutionize parenting around the world. She has a passion for making a difference in the lives of women and children and travels nationally as a parenting and relationship expert. Dawn is a highly sought-after speaker and trainer who specializes in entitlement issues that are currently plaguing our society.

Dawn has a master's degree in Clinical Psychology, while her doctorate studies focus on organizational psychology and personality. She is also the author of over twenty books. Dawn is also the President of Dawn L. Billings, Inc. a training and executive coaching company where she is a consultant to executives and organizations focusing on teamwork, communication skills, improving productivity, and retaining top talent. Dawn is the creator and author of an amazingly simple but powerful assessment tool known as the "Primary Colors Personality Test." Dawn's personality test was administered to over sixty thousand couples and families in 2007 and even more than that in 2008. The test helps couples communicate better with each other and with their children.

Dawn Billings

3433 Kenwood Street
Mesa, AZ 85213
918-605-1492
theheartlink@aol.com
www.TheHeartLinkNetwork.com
www.TROVAWomenBusinessDirectory.com
www.GetCapables.com
www.Heart-Notes.com
www.TheHeartAlliance.com
www.DawnBillings.com

CHAPTER SEVEN

Having Fun in Business

An interview with...

S. David Drewelow

DAVID WRIGHT (WRIGHT)

Today we're talking with David Drewelow. David grew up with an entrepreneurial dad who owned multiple businesses that sparked his desire to start his first company, a successful painting business, while still in college. Today he is an owner of an ActionCOACH master franchise where he is a franchise developer and recruiter to bring coaches into the ActionCOACH network. He also owns a Web marketing company, actively serves on several boards, is a motivational speaker, coach and a leadership trainer. His work focuses on helping business coaches, business owners, associations, and non-profit organizations. David's passion is to help others achieve their dream of business ownership and to help owners connect with the concept of having "fun" in business. He uses his life and professional experience from his thirty-five-year career that includes advertising, sales, radio, media consulting, non-profit leadership, training, web marketing, and business coaching.

David Drewelow, welcome to *GPS to Success: Goals and Proven Strategies*.

S. DAVID DREWELOW (DREWELOW)

Thank you, pleasure to be with you.

WRIGHT

So why is having fun business and life, for that matter, so important to you?

DREWELOW

Well, my dad was a business guy and the father of eight children and he said that the only way he could make enough money for his big family was to own his own business. He said there was no job that could do this for him, plus he thought it was important to enjoy whatever work or business he was in. If, when he got up in the morning, he looked in the mirror and was dreading going to work, then he would say, "why do it?"

I've carried that with me for years. I believe that whatever it is we do if we can't enjoy it, then maybe we need to do something different. I find it interesting how people react when I say, "You can have fun in business." They think I'm crazy or something—being in business can't be fun!

WRIGHT

So has being in business always been fun for you?

DREWELOW

No, not always. It is about your perspective and your attitude, and we'll talk about some things regarding failure and success. Obviously, we learn more from our failures, but there have been times, I must admit when business has not been fun.

The economy downturn has presented many challenges. I believe, however, that it is how we react to things, rather than letting our circumstances dictate our attitude when it comes to "fun." So, no, business is not always fun, however it depends on your perspective and your attitude.

WRIGHT

You say that having fun is based on six key points to define the culture of your business. Would you tell our readers what those points are?

DREWELOW

Sure. I think it starts with the owner or leader of the business. I work with people helping them to define the culture of their business and at the same time I help them to become a better leader. A "culture" exists in every business, but many business owners don't always think about their culture. It starts with them as leaders and it is their responsibility to clearly identify the culture they want in their business. This is all about good leadership, and I see that as the first thing.

Your culture should also allow people the opportunity to fail. You need to give them the freedom and flexibility, with parameters, to fail. Some people need to fail because it is the best way for them to learn. This also includes minimizing the "I know" attitude that can sometimes dominate what's going on in your business. This negative attitude impacts morale and can dampen the opportunity to learn from failure. Learning from failure allows your culture to promote ongoing learning.

Your culture should also promote "above the line" behavior in people. Do they blame others or do they take responsibility for their words and actions? Clearly, laying out expectations will greatly improve your culture. Obviously, every business wants to have a winning team—a team that is motivated and driven for success, and one that is fun and enjoyable to work with. And a key factor in all of this with your culture is having excellent communication. We will talk more about this later in this chapter, but really understanding the absolute importance of having excellent communication is a critical component of your culture.

And finally, the last point around culture (and this is a biggie for me) is all about attitude—having the right attitude. When all of these elements are a part of your culture in a place of business or work environment, then it really can be a lot more fun.

WRIGHT

Why should defining the culture of business be important to people?

DREWELOW

I have found that a lot of people who own businesses seem to be in denial when it comes to truly identifying their culture. I've seen this with clients I've worked with where the owner does not really understand what's going on in their business. They don't realize that they set the tone and they set the bar for their people. They don't understand that culture starts at the top with them. They don't see what they are creating and how it influences their people. This is huge, it's critical.

The first thing is to focus on working with people or owners to get them to define what their culture is all about. Sometimes it takes a lot of work and I will suggest the owner take a weekend getaway to sit down and really take a look at what's going on in his or her business. This is important and once owners figure this out, then they have a much better shot at getting their entire team on the same page. Many employees can tell you what their culture is all about, but sometimes the owner just doesn't see it.

WRIGHT

How would you define "culture"?

DREWELOW

Culture is the environment, what goes on, the expectations, the value system, and the beliefs of the owner. I make it clear, for example, with my business so my people know the things I believe. Within the ActionCOACH franchise we have our "14 Points of Culture." These points list expectations and areas where we will operate from that include integrity, honesty, excellence, communication, team, gratitude, having fun, and more. I am really surprised that many businesses don't do this.

WRIGHT

So your next point is to allow people to fail. How can failure actually contribute to fun?

DREWELOW

When I'm speaking to a group, I tell them to think about a time when they experienced failure. Of course, it was not necessarily fun at the moment, however, the situation may be funny later when they tell the story about something really dumb they did and how they learned from that experience.

I think of my dad. He was the sales guy for all of his businesses and he would tell stories about his door-to-door experiences. He sold encyclopedias, insurance, siding, and many other things. Of course, selling door-to-door, he had many an experience with dogs. Quite often during those moments he was not having fun and felt like a failure because he could not get to the door of the house. However, he learned to turn it into a positive in that the dog would serve as a "screener" for the owner—an effective way to keep the sales guy away. He looked at every dog as a way to allow him more time for other calls where he did not have to deal with roadblocks.

Was this from failure to fun, maybe? It is an attitude adjustment. My dad would take bad situations—times when he was not successful—and turn them into learning experiences and fun stories.

WRIGHT

You mentioned the "I know" attitude that people sometimes have. How have you seen that attitude affect a business?

DREWELOW

The biggest thing is getting people to actually admit when they have a negative attitude. We all know teenagers who are, to most, guilty culprits—they know it all, just ask them! However, for many people it does not go away when they become adults. When we get older we often simply become more discreet and we cover it up.

When I am working with business owners and their teams, I get them to open up and see when someone has an "I know" attitude. I stress that you can't tell the "I know" people anything, you can't teach them anything, and often you can't even get them to even listen when they have an "I know" attitude. It is a very difficult situation. It is all about the six inches between their ears that seems to be the biggest challenge. If somebody seems to have all the answers, then he or she will be very difficult to work with. I have found that the older I get, the more I don't know.

For a young person, if we can get them to open up their mind, then maybe we have a shot at teaching them something. Some believe that graduating from high school or college is the end of learning, but in reality it should be the beginning. Learning is a lifelong process. I stress to clients that they should encourage ongoing learning, looking for people who love to learn—people who see huge value in doing things to improve themselves. When you get people on board with this idea, then it can really change the environment within a business.

WRIGHT

If I was taking notes correctly your fourth point was to make sure people operate above the line. Will you explain how the line—the "decision line" as you call it—works to help businesses, leaders, and their teams?

DREWELOW

This principle is all about having the right attitude. We first encourage leaders to teach their people the importance of knowing what below-the-line behavior looks like. We start by asking people what they believe operating below the line means. They quickly understand and will come up with definitions such as blaming other people, making excuses for why they didn't get something done, or maybe the person is even in denial and he or she is part of the problem. Many below-the-line people have an entitlement mentality, and yes, unfortunately we have way too much of that in our culture today! This is not only a workplace issue, but can be a family issue as well.

Once they know what not to do, then we talk about the positive, which is above-the-line behavior. When people operate above the line, they are willing to take ownership for the things they do and they are willing to take responsibility for their actions and the things they say. Even further, they're willing to allow others to hold them accountable for those behaviors. They are willing to use a set of standards to operate within.

Above-the-line mentality is really about having the right attitude and it can be a very powerful thing. When people start to see the value based on results, they begin to enjoy this principle. Sometimes people say they don't want somebody running around as the self-appointed "line" police. We all dip below the line on occasion and have a bad attitude, and maybe we even blame someone else for things we should own. If we can get people to see the value and get their businesses and their people to understand and agree to stay above that line, then it will have a huge affect on that environment. And that makes it more fun.

WRIGHT

Why do you think the decision line is so powerful?

DREWELOW

It comes down to personal responsibility—people having or understanding that it is their decision and it is their responsibility to decide their attitude. They must make a decision every day to have the right attitude. It is that simple. So, when people have a bad yesterday, they can choose to pick themselves right back up with a better attitude. I like to tell people that you are not allowed to have a bad day; but rather, you are only allowed to have a bad hour. After that you need to get over it and move on.

The decision line is all about attitude, and each person has the responsibility for what his or her attitude is going to be.

WRIGHT

You're fifth point in defining the culture of a business is to build a winning team. Will you explain each of those points?

DREWELOW

Sure. I believe that having a winning team makes all the difference in a business; having a winning team starts with strong leadership. John Maxwell is one of my favorite leadership guys; he says, "... everything rises and falls on leadership." If somebody thinks he or she is the leader and turns around and sees nobody is following, then the leader is simply out for a walk. According to Maxwell these kinds of leaders are most likely not leading anyone, except for maybe themselves, and they are probably not doing a very good job of that! So, the first key point is having a strong leader. I have worked with business owners who don't really want to be the leader and they cannot make a decision. Well, in my opinion, if you own the business then you have to be the leader, or you need to get somebody in charge of running the place who is.

Number two is having a common goal and communicating that common goal to all of your people. Many times I've worked with people who have an idea of what they want their business to accomplish but they haven't shared it with their team, which makes it difficult for them. The team cannot take ownership and they don't feel as though they are invested in what is going on in the business until they know the common goal.

The third is to understand the rules of the game in the business. The rules state what everyone is allowed to do, what are they not allowed to do, and what their roles are going to be in helping the business to achieve its goals. Having rules and guidelines is very important. The team members need to know what exactly they can do that will allow them to participate and be a part of the business in order for it to be successful.

The next key to a winning team is having a plan. Without a plan, many businesses take on a "ready-shoot-aim" mentality. They just react to business. Many owners do not have a long-term plan. We begin by introducing short-term planning that will become part of their business development process. It is important to have an action plan that is very clearly defined as well as defining the roles of each of the team members in order for them to be able to execute their part of the plan.

Another critical component to building a winning team is having a business owner or leader who supports risk-taking with his or her people. People need to know (again, back to the rules) what they can do or not do. They need to know if they make a risky decision that does not work out, the leader will still support them. Granted, parameters must be in place, but owners have to allow people to take some risks; it would not be wise to jump all over them if they make a decision that fails. If you do, then they will never make a risky decision again. Allowing your people to take risks and supporting them through the learning experiences of failure is very important.

The last key point has a couple of elements to it. The first is inclusion, which is the responsibility of the owner. This means that owners must include their people in what's going on in the business and this happens with good communication. In fact, communication is the "glue" that brings all of these six points together with a winning team. The second part of this is the responsibility of the team members or the employees, which is 100% involvement. Simply put, people must show up for work every day with a willingness to give their very best, at 100 percent, to the team and to the business.

WRIGHT

Your final point is about attitude and that it is a part of the first five. Why is attitude so important, in your opinion?

DREWELOW

I used to say in my younger days that attitude is half the battle. One day somebody challenged me and asked why I called it a "battle" because it sounded too negative. I thought about it and decided that having a good attitude needed to be based on a positive.

I did some research and some rethinking; then I realized that your attitude is all about making a decision. As Chuck Swindoll says, "It is not what happens to you, but how you react to what happens to you is what determines your attitude." I enjoy people who have a positive attitude and I get a kick out of those who are eternal optimists. According to my wife, I am an EO—an eternal optimist—sometimes to a fault. When people have a great attitude, their attitude shows up before they do! Do you know what I mean? Have you ever met that Eeyore type of person who walks around with a cloud over his or her head? Everything is woe is me, doom and gloom. Quite honestly, these are not fun people to be around. When people have a great attitude and are optimistic about what's going on, it circles back around to this whole concept of having fun in business and in your work. I really think attitude is *the* big point and what it's all about.

WRIGHT

Do you believe you can have fun and still be serious in business?

DREWELOW

Absolutely. Again, having fun means you will follow guidelines and rules and procedures and we find best practices.

I used to be involved in a many different kinds of sports; I'm a very competitive person. People will say, "We're just out here to have fun."

My reply to that is, "Well you know what? I have a lot more fun when I'm winning than when I'm losing."

It's the same thing in business. Whether it be accomplishing goals or accomplishing a mission, I believe that a good business deserves to be profitable, but it needs to be a good sound business. So yes, it is more fun if you're successful versus if you are not. Right now, with the economy the way it is, this is a huge issue.

My focus is to help people to have more fun in business while still understanding the importance of using best practices and following systems and processes as well as the basic rules of the game to be successful. When people are successful they will have more fun.

WRIGHT

Well, what an interesting conversation. Fun in business—that's great. Sometimes I've had fun in business and sometimes it hasn't been so much fun. That's why I've been listening very intently here to maybe turn my work into more fun.

I really appreciate all the time you've taken to answer these questions. I have learned a lot here today and I'm sure our readers will as well.

DREWELOW

Excellent. Thank you very much for your time also.

WRIGHT

Today we've been talking with David Drewelow. David is the owner of an ActionCOACH master franchise as a franchise developer and recruiter to bring coaches into the ActionCOACH Network and to assist business owners toward growing their businesses. His passion is, as we have discovered here today, is to help others to achieve their dreams of business ownership and to help others connect to the concept of having fun in business. After listening to him I think he knows what he's talking about.

David, thank you so much for being with us today on *GPS to Success: Goals and Proven Strategies.*

DREWELOW

My pleasure; I've enjoyed it.

About the Author

David Drewelow is a business owner and master franchisor for the ActionCOACH USA Heartland Region with offices in Iowa, Nebraska, Missouri, and Kansas. He is a business coach, public speaker, franchise specialist, and team trainer. He also has interests in two other businesses.

David is the past president of the North American Master Coaches Association, director for the International Business Coach Institute, and is involved in regional chambers, economic development groups, and civic, charitable, and Christian organizations.

Prior to business ownership, his background included non-profit leadership, business development, training, media research, ad agencies, and radio and television. He is a University of Northern Iowa graduate in Radio/TV Speech, Journalism, and Business.

David is married to his very best friend, Lonna, and they have two sons, a favorite daughter-in-law, and his grandkids are a blast! David's mission in life is *"to glorify God while helping people achieve their dreams!"*

S. David Drewelow

ActionCOACH USA Heartland Region
Heartland Business Coaching, LLC
DNA Concepts Web-Marketing-Coaching
417 1st Ave SE, Suite 215
Cedar Rapids, IA 52401
319-743-0642
david@drewelow.com
www.daviddrewelow.com
www.dnaconcepts.net

CHAPTER EIGHT
Stretch, Push Yourself, and Reach Further

An interview with...
Les Brown

DAVID WRIGHT (WRIGHT)

Today we're talking with Les Brown, internationally recognized speaker and CEO of Les Brown Enterprises, Inc. He is also author of the highly acclaimed and successful books, *Live Your Dreams* and *It's Not Over Until You Win*. Les is former host of the *Les Brown Show,* a nationally syndicated daily television talk show that focused on solutions rather than on problems. Les Brown is one of the nation's leading authorities on understanding and stimulating human potential. Utilizing powerful delivery and newly emerging insights, Les's customized presentations will teach, inspire, and channel any audience to new levels of achievement.

Les Brown, welcome to *GPS for Success: Goals and Proven Strategies.*

LES BROWN (BROWN)

Thank you very much. It's a pleasure to be here.

WRIGHT

Les, you've been a role model for thousands of people down through the years because of your triumph over adversity. Tell our readers a little bit about your early life and who was responsible for your upbringing.

BROWN

Well, I was born in a poor section of Miami, Florida, called Liberty City. I was born on the floor of an abandoned building along with a twin brother. When we were six weeks of age, we were adopted. When I was in the fifth grade I was identified as EMR (Educable Mentally Retarded) and put back into the fourth grade. I failed again when I was in the eighth grade.

I attribute everything that I've accomplished to my mother. Whenever I give a presentation I always quote Abraham Lincoln by saying, "All that I am and all that I ever hope to be, I owe to my mother." I saw a sign once that said, "God took me out of my biological mother's womb and placed me in the heart of my adopted mother." I love my adopted mother's faith, her character, her drive, her dedication, and her willingness to do whatever it took to raise seven children by herself. She only had a third grade education but she had a Ph.D. in mothering.

WRIGHT

If I remember correctly, you were diagnosed at the age of thirty-six with dyslexia. How did that happen?

BROWN

No, I was never diagnosed with dyslexia; but I was in special education from fourth grade all the way through my senior year in high school. My formal education ended at that time; but I became very much interested in personal development tapes and books because of a high school teacher who challenged me to do something in a class. I told him I couldn't do it and he insisted that I could.

Finally, I said, "I can't because I'm Educable Mentally Retarded."

He said, "Don't ever say that again. Someone's opinion of you does not have to become your reality."

This teacher's name was Mr. Leroy Washington and he's still around today. One of the things he emphasized to all of his students was that you don't get in life what you *want*—you get in life what you *are*. What you achieve—what you produce in life—is a reflection of your growth and development as a person. So you must invest in yourself.

He often quoted scripture by saying, "Be ye not conformed to this world: but be ye transformed by the renewing of your mind . . . " (Romans 12:2). He said most people fail in life because "they don't know that they don't know and they think they know"—they suffer from mental malnutrition. He said take the time each day to develop your mind, read ten to fifteen pages of something positive every day, and find some goals that are beyond your comfort zone that can challenge you to reinvent yourself. He told his students that in order to do something you've never done, you've got to be someone you've never been. He told us the possibilities of what you could achieve by developing your mind and developing your communication skills (because once you open your mouth you tell the world who you are). You can really begin to climb the ladder of success and do things that will literally amaze you.

WRIGHT

So your education is self-education.

BROWN

Yes.

WRIGHT

Listening to tapes and reading books and that sort of thing?

BROWN

Yes. Going to seminars and then testing and experimenting. I think it's very important that people experiment with their lives and find out what it is that works for them—what gives their lives a sense of joy and meaning. What is it that brings music to your life? That way you're able to discover some talents, abilities, and skills you don't even realize you have.

WRIGHT

I remember reading your first book, *Live Your Dreams*. This bestseller is helping people even today. Can you tell us what you're trying to say in this book and why it is important?

BROWN

What I'm doing in *Live Your Dreams* is challenging people to look at their situation and ask themselves some crucial questions. Is life working for me? Is it really giving me what I want?

When most people get out of high school, they end up doing things that other people want them to do. Albert Schweitzer was asked a question, "What's wrong with humankind today?" He replied, "Men simply don't think." He meant that statement in a generic sense. Men *and* women simply don't challenge themselves to think about what it is that really makes them happy and gives their lives a sense of meaning, purpose, power, and value.

I want to challenge people to think about what it is that really gives their lives a sense of meaning and power. Once you determine that, assess yourself. What are your strengths? What are your weaknesses? What is it you bring to the table of life? What help? What assistance? What training? What education? What resources? What do you have to tap into that will help you to become the kind of person that can produce those results?

Then next is to commit yourself. Don't ask yourself, "How am I going to do it?" The "how" is none of your business—what is most important is to get started—the how will come. The way will come. Everything you need to attract—the people, the resources, and the assistance—will come to be available at your disposal.

WRIGHT

What do you think about goal-setting? There has been so much written about it lately.

BROWN

I think it's very important that people set goals because what that does is allow you to focus your energy. It helps you to put together a game plan and a strategy and an agenda for your life. If you don't have an agenda for your life, then you're going to be a part of somebody else's agenda; therefore, you want to set some goals. There's a quote I love very much that says, "People who aim at nothing in life usually hit nothing dead on the head."

WRIGHT

Oh, my.

BROWN

Yes, so you want to have some goals you are setting in each area of your life. You want to monitor those goals after you put together a plan of action to achieve those goals. Break those goals down into manageable increments: long-range and short-range goals, three-month goals, thirty-day goals, and weekly goals. You should have daily tasks and activities you engage in that will move you in the direction of your goals. Dr. Robert H. Schuller said something that is true, "By the yard it's hard, but inch by inch anything is a cinch."

As you begin to look at the big picture and come back to where you are right now, looking at the completed big picture of where you want to go, then you can begin to put together a strategy of things and activities you need to do each day to move you in the direction of those goals. As you get closer to those goals you have set for yourself in the various areas of your life—your physical life, your emotional life, your spiritual life, your financial life—then you can begin to push the goals back. Continue to stretch—continue to push yourself—and reach farther.

WRIGHT

A few years ago you had a nationally syndicated television talk show. It's next to impossible to get a show of that nature on the air. Tell us the circumstances that helped to get your show on the air.

BROWN

I believe I'm coming back, I don't think it's impossible to get back on again. I wanted to go in a different direction. During the time I ventured into it, television was based upon a formula the executives were accustomed to which they'd always implemented—the show must be based upon conflict and controversy. So you had Phil Donahue, Oprah Winfrey, Sally Jesse Raphael, and Geraldo. My show was based upon solutions. I believed you could have a show that was not based upon conflict and controversy—you could have a show where you would look at what challenges people are facing and who has gone through a challenge and come out on the other side? Talk to that person and find out how he or she got there. Interview a guest who is in the middle of a challenge and find one who's just approaching that challenge. Have an expert work the person through that process during the hour of the show, asking what is it that brought you here? There's an old saying that goes, "Wherever you find yourself, at some point and time, you made an appointment to get there."

The other thing is that success leaves clues. What we must do is talk to someone who's had the same problem you've had and find out from his or her experience what is it you can do to implement a game plan. What help and support will you need to work through this problem?

The *Les Brown Show* was very successful. It was the highest rated and fastest cancelled talk show in the history of television. It was cancelled because, even though it had successful ratings, the producers of the show wanted me to do a show based upon conflict and controversy and sensationalism—fathers who sleep with their fourteen-year-old daughter's boyfriends—and subjects like that. I decided to be true to my concept and not venture off into those other areas to do those Jerry Springer type shows, so they cancelled the show and brought someone else in who was willing to cooperate with what they wanted.

WRIGHT

Did you learn any lessons from your highly competitive talk show?

BROWN

Yes I did. The lesson I learned was I should have been the executive producer. I was hired talent and "the hand that pays the piper calls the tune." Had I been the executive producer of my show like Oprah Winfrey, then I could have done what Oprah did after she saw the success of my show—she changed direction and used the formula I'd come up with and the rest is history.

If I had it to do over again I would've put my own production company together, continued to do the show I was doing, and would've found someone else to syndicate the show nationally. If I couldn't find someone to syndicate the show nationally I would've set it up to do it locally and then rolled it back out nationally myself.

WRIGHT

I bet you still get stopped on the street by people who saw your commercials on the PBS station for many years. Those were some of the best produced I've ever seen.

BROWN

Well, thank you. We've gotten a lot of response from PBS. We just did one show four months ago called, *It's in Your Hands*. In fact, I end the show with my children because five of my seven children are speakers as well; they're also trainers. What we're doing is teaching people how to become responsible for their careers, their health, and for their family life. The response has been very, very successful on PBS.

WRIGHT

So you're growing your own speakers, then.

BROWN

Yes, and I'm training speakers—I'm more of a speech coach. I've developed a reputation as a speaker, but I have a gift of helping people tell their story and to position it so it has value for an audience. I have people's stories create special, magical moments within the context of their presentation so that those stories can create a committed listening audience and move them to new heights within themselves.

WRIGHT

Yes, you don't have to tell me you're a sought-after speaker. Some time ago we were planning a speaking engagement in Ohio and the two people who were requested more than any others were Stephen Covey and Les Brown. They really came after you, so you do have quite a reputation for helping people.

BROWN

Thank you.

WRIGHT

A lot of our readers have read many books that advocate focus in their career. I know you've done several things and you've done them well. Do you advocate going in one direction and not diversifying in your career?

BROWN

I think that you have to find one area you want to focus on and as you develop momentum in that area and reach a certain measure of success, then you can branch off into other areas.

WRIGHT

Les, you had a serious bout with cancer several years ago, right?

BROWN

Yes.

WRIGHT

How did this catastrophic disease affect your life?

BROWN

What cancer did for me was help me live life with a sense of urgency that tomorrow is not guaranteed. It helped me reprioritize my life and find out what's really important. When something major like cancer happens in your life, you spend more time focusing on those things. So, even though I always practiced and advocated that people live each day as if it were their last, my cancer battle helped me to focus even more so on priorities. That's what I began to be about the business of doing— thinking about my legacy, spending more time with my children, my grandchildren, friends I cared about, and working on the purpose I've embraced for my life.

WRIGHT

My wife was going through cancer at the same time you were, I remember. I heard her say recently that even though she doesn't want cancer again, she wouldn't give anything for the lessons she learned going through it.

BROWN

Yes. It helps; it gives new meaning to life, and you value things you used to take for granted.

WRIGHT

So, you gained a lot of insight into what's important?

BROWN

Oh, without any question I did.

WRIGHT

Your book, *It's Not Over Until You Win*, was long awaited, of course. Would you tell our readers what it's about and what you're trying to say?

BROWN

I think what people must do is challenge themselves to overcome the inner conversation that has been placed in them through their conditioning, through their environment, and their circumstances. We live in a world where we're told more about our limitations rather than our potential. We need to overcome and defeat that conversation.

If you ask most people if they have ever been told they can't achieve a goal they envision for their life will say, "Yes." My whole goal is to help people learn how to become unstoppable. Yes, it's going to be difficult—it's going to be hard. You're going to have obstacles thrown in your path. You will have setbacks and disappointments. But you must develop the mind-set of a winner. You must come back again and again and again. You must be creative and flexible, versatile and adaptable, and never stop until you reach your goals.

WRIGHT

I read many years ago that 98 percent of all failure comes from quitting. Would you agree with that?

BROWN

Yes, I agree with that without any question. Most people become discouraged and they see delay as a denial. I encourage people to go back to the drawing board in their minds, regroup, and get some fresh thinking. Einstein said, "The thinking that has brought me this far has created some problems that this thinking can't solve."

Sometimes we have to allow other people to be a part of the process—to look at the situation we're battling with new eyes that can help us overcome the challenges we're facing.

WRIGHT

As I have said before, you have been a role model for thousands of adults as well as young people. Do you have any advice to give our readers that would help them to grow in body, mind, and spirit and live a better, fuller life?

BROWN

Yes. I think it's important for people to raise the bar on themselves every day. Look at your life and understand and know you are greater than you give yourself credit for being; you have talents and abilities you haven't even begun to reach for yet.

Jim Rohn has a quote I love, "When the end comes for you, let it find you conquering a new mountain, not sliding down an old one." So, therefore, we have to raise the bar on ourselves constantly and assess ourselves.

The other thing is I believe it's important we ask for help, not because we're weak but because we want to remain strong. Many people don't ask for help because of pride. "Pride cometh before a fall" because of ego. E-G-O means edging God out.

I think that you also have to ask yourself, what is your plan for being here? Most people take their health for granted; but living a long, healthy life is not a given—pain is a given—you have to fight to stay here. You have to have a plan of action to stay here. So what is your plan for being here? Put yourself on your to-do list. Develop a plan of action on how you're going to take better care of yourself and spend more time with people you care about. Focus on living the goals and dreams you've envisioned for yourself that are the calling on your life.

WRIGHT

Down through the years, as you've made your decisions, has faith played an important role in your life?

BROWN

Yes, faith is very important. I think you have to believe in yourself, believe in your abilities, believe in your dreams, and believe in a power greater than yourself. There's a quote I love which says, "Faith is the oil that takes the friction out of living." Do the best you can and leave the rest to a power greater than yourself.

WRIGHT

Les, you don't know how much I appreciate you being with us today for *GPS for Success: Goals and Proven Strategies.*

BROWN

Oh, thank you so much.

WRIGHT

Today we've been talking with Les Brown, an internationally recognized speaker and CEO of Les Brown Enterprises. He's the author of *Live Your Dreams* and *It's Not Over Until You Win*. I suggest you run down to the bookstore and look for both of them. Les has been a successful talk show host and as we have heard today, he is now coaching speakers.

Thank you so much for being with us, Les.

BROWN

Thank you, I appreciate you very much.

ABOUT THE AUTHOR

Les Brown is an internationally recognized speaker and CEO of Les Brown Enterprises, Inc. He is also author of the highly acclaimed and successful books, *Live Your Dreams* and *It's Not Over Until You Win*. Les Brown is one of the nation's leading authorities in understanding and stimulating human potential.

Les Brown
Les Brown Enterprises
P.O. Box 27380
Detroit, Michigan 48227
800-733-4226
speak@lesbrown.com
www.lesbrown.com

CHAPTER NINE
Building Castle Walls to Stand On

An interview with...

Kate Michels

DAVID WRIGHT (WRIGHT)

Today we're talking to Kate Michels. Kate is a popular, renowned and respectfully established veteran practitioner, trainer, and instructor in the field of self-help and life coaching. She has been personally and professionally committed to "life coaching" tools since she was introduced to some of the great masters of this movement such as Milton Erickson and the "I'm Okay and You're Okay" principles in high school. Her commitment to people living up to their full potential reaches from pregnant women and their newborn infants to those who have committed crimes and are presently doing time. Creator, designer, facilitator, and chief instructor of Core Alignment Coaching, Kate is the best-selling author of several books, a sought-after motivational speaker, and a "Wake Up woman," She is also a representative of the Summer of Peace, Center Point's LPIP Answer Woman, an "amazing dreamer," and a successful Real Estate broker in Portland, Oregon.

Kate is also a wife, mother, daughter, sister, and grandmother. Her commitment to the principle that everyone is whole, perfect, creative, and resourceful in making the best decisions with the information he or she currently has, leads to her continued pursuit of gathering information. Kate has had lasting results from everything from bi-polar anxiety issues, eating disorders, sleep issues, and struggles of everyday living.

Kate welcome to *GPS to Success: Goals and Proven Strategies.*

KATE MICHELS (MICHELS)

Thank you, glad to be here and excited to support others in setting their goals and developing their personal strategies.

WRIGHT

You're coaching practice is called Castle-Building. Where did this name come from?

MICHELS

When I graduated from the Erickson International Coaching Program, I was approached by Marilyn Atkinson, the founder, and invited to come with her to Prague to represent America as a trainer of trainers internationally. At that time she said we would be leaving in three weeks—twenty-one days. I told her that I had no birth certificate, no passport, and didn't think I would be able to go, but I appreciated the offer.

"Well," she replied, "if you aren't interested in playing this big game with me, that's your choice."

I then went home and mentioned this to my husband who said, "Well, it does sound like too good a game to pass up!"

So I decided to see what I could do. I called the travel agent who told me it would take a miracle for me to make it to Prague in 21 days. Well, twenty-three days later I found myself standing on top of a castle wall in Sylvania, which is near Prague. I looked around and said, "Castles are built from knowing what you want, from asking for it, being willing, being persistent, and from being grateful." That's how castles are built and that's how Castle Building Coaching was formed. From that castle wall (still standing here after hundreds of years), I looked around the countryside and proclaimed loudly, "Wow, miracles do happen every day," and I proclaim that now daily.

WRIGHT

So how do you support people by, as you say, building castles?

MICHELS

I recognize that within all of us there exists the potential to get anything we want. Everyone has that ability—each one of us is born with our purpose, our essence, and our gifts. Simply by standing in that truth and knowing our value, we begin to receive everything we ask for. We begin to live the life we love, do whatever we want, and build the castles of our lives. There are five steps I use along the way to, as I say, "have miracles happen every day."

WRIGHT

Are you saying that this is about having success in one's life, reaching one's potential, or as you have said, miracles happen every day?

MICHELS

Yes, it's about recognizing our potential; it's about living true to ourselves, having our success, setting goals, and recognizing that miracles happen every day. I don't mean the miracles of the rainbows that come after the flood, I mean the miracles that come in the floods, and the challenges that transform us, change us, and propel us. Like my getting to Prague; there were obstacles that stood in my way and I could have easily said, "Oh well, thank you very much," but instead, I knew what I wanted and I began moving toward it using the five simple steps I will mention that lead to miracles happen every day and castles being built.

WRIGHT

So what are those five steps exactly?

MICHELS

The first step is to know what you want. The second step is to ask for it, not just ask yourself, but ask everyone you can think of, including the universe. The third step is to begin showing up to receive what you want. People often ask, and they could get it but they just don't show up to get it. The fourth step is to keep your word. The fifth step, which I also say is the first step and necessary with every step, is the natural attitude of gratitude.

WRIGHT

So the first is to know what it is that one really wants. How do people find out exactly what they really do want?

MICHELS

Well, people often think they know what they want and they begin to move in that direction. They find themselves years later wondering where they have spent the last few years of their journey because they're not any closer to getting what they thought they wanted when they started.

To know what we really want we must know who we really are and what our core values are. This is the chunked up principle of standing in the light of what we will get when we get what we want. So it's more than just, "I want to make money," it's if you make money, what will you then do? "Oh, well, if I make money then I'll be able to live free." If you're free what will you then do? "Well, I would spread the message of peace to the world." Oh, so that's what you really want—to spread the message of peace to the world. That's standing on the true value of what one really wants.

WRIGHT

So the next step that you mention is asking, who does one ask?

MICHELS

This is really important because we will often begin to know what we want but not be willing to step out and ask. There is a well known principle that we are usually only five places or people away from getting what we really want. So I suggest that people ask everyone they know, tell everyone they know, and find all of the people they know and ask them for support. It is also important to ask themselves, on a consistent and regular basis, if they are still going in the right direction. Mainly though, ask the universe, trusting that the universe can deliver and can do so much quicker than we usually can.

WRIGHT

Then the next step you mention is showing up to get it. What do you mean, when you say just "show up"?

MICHELS

Showing up means actually being there—all of you with all you offer and all you have to give. People will often know what they want, they'll ask for it, and then when it comes right down to it—to actually taking the steps—they just won't do it.

Similar to my trip to Prague, the steps were possible and I could choose to take the steps or not take the steps. To get my passport I had to show up in Seattle, stand there, get my picture taken, and be handed my passport so I could make it in twenty-one days. I actually had to show up in person to receive the miracle and the blessings. So what I mean is to stand up, asking what you ask for, taking the steps, and showing up to get it all the time, every day, every morning when you wake up.

WRIGHT

The fourth step is keeping one's word, which sounds like a really big one to me. Would you tell our readers more about what keeping one's word is all about?

MICHELS

This is vital. Keeping our word is really important, especially to ourselves. When we know who we are, know what we really want, know our value, and begin to show up in a greater way to the world, it's even more important that we keep our word. If we say we're going to be somewhere, we need to be there. If we say we want to be invited, then when we're invited, we need to go. If we're offered an invitation, we need to accept that invitation.

The universe is often extending to us the opportunity to get what we want; we miss that opportunity by just not showing up and by not keeping our word. You never know where the next miracle might be. So you want to keep your word, not just to people, not just to yourself, but also to the universe as a whole. Saying yes is one thing, doing yes is the big thing.

WRIGHT

The fifth step, as you say, is a natural attitude of gratitude. How does someone do this step, or is it just something that happens?

MICHELS

The natural attitude of gratitude is something that just naturally happens, and as I say, it's the fifth step. People can also increase their natural attitude of gratitude. As I mentioned before, in the miracles that happen, it might not be the rainbow, it might be the flood. If we have a natural attitude of gratitude, then even when the floods show up, we know that this will serve us—this is something that has been brought to us with a positive intention and all things work for the good.

So in all moments, in all experiences, in all that presents itself we show up—every time we keep our word with gratitude. Then we will have a natural attitude of gratitude, trusting that things are working out the way that they have been planned for us and getting us what we really want. We are moving along daily living true to ourselves and having that natural attitude of gratitude.

WRIGHT

By putting this in your fifth step, it's almost as if you think that people are not naturally grateful. Does gratitude not come naturally or is it something that we have to work on?

MICHELS

It does come naturally and it is something that we want to be working on as well. As we recognize that we're getting closer and closer to what we want, if we keep that natural attitude of gratitude, then we'll count our blessings. As we count our blessings our value will increase, and as our value increases our opportunity to receive more of what we want will be achieved.

As I mentioned in the beginning, that's how castles are built. Castles are built by knowing, by asking, by being willing, by being persistent, and by being grateful. Focus on what you are getting and you will naturally get more, thus you will have more to be grateful for. All of this is natural, yet you are consciously doing it.

WRIGHT

It's said by many people, and there are many books on it now, that the generation just now coming out of college and out of high school going into the workforce have an attitude of entitlement. They're going to have to really work on an attitude of gratitude. Wouldn't you think?

MICHELS

One of the things that the attitude of entitlement does is decreases one's value. It begins to make someone believe that life is happening to them, instead of their being proactive and making things happen for them. We are each one of us creating or building our own castle, and if we have an attitude of entitlement we miss out on who we are and what we're capable of doing. Entitlement misses the value our essence, purpose, and gifts we bring to others. We are here to build the castle walls that will be standing hundreds of years for others to stand upon and see their castles being built.

WRIGHT

Well stated. So are these five steps done at one time in a linear fashion? What is the best way to follow the steps?

MICHELS

As I mentioned before, that natural attitude of gratitude coming as the first step, is one of the best ways to go. Remind yourself of these five steps on a consistent basis and do all of them always. I do know that miracles happen every day when we stand in the principle of 1) knowing what we want, 2) asking for what we want, 3) showing up to get it, 4) keeping our word, and 5) having a natural attitude of gratitude. Knowing these five steps, doing them, and moving in that direction always gets us there. It isn't linear, yet the steps are supportive linearly.

There might be a time when we're included in something, keep our word, and wow, a miracle happens. We show up for ourselves and a miracle happens. Another time we might be thinking about not doing something that we told someone we would do, and if we know "wow, a miracle might not happen if I don't keep my word," we are going to keep our word. So not only are these principles supportive in a linear fashion, they are also supportive in an individual fashion. A castle is built with a plan, one stone at a time. Being willing to make changes along the way deepens what is supplied by the universe. Be grateful, show up, keep your word, know what you want and ask for it. In any order, it works.

WRIGHT

So would you tell our readers what happens next after the castle is built?

MICHELS

Another miracle happens. It's like my getting to Prague and standing on that castle wall. It was the first castle I had ever seen. It had been built on the ruins of four previous castles. Upon every castle we build, another castle will be built. So you build your first castle and you build upon it. Build the next castle and you build upon that one and so on. Then others will come and build upon what you have built.

Throughout our life we are offered many visions; those visions are building toward our mission. Our mission is highlighted by our essence and our essence comes from our purpose. For me, my purpose is to highlight the miracles of everyday living. My essence is in recognizing the potential of miracles happening for everyone, and all of my castles are built upon those precepts.

WRIGHT

Is this a euphemism for goal-setting?

MICHELS

It is. Castle-building is one way to describe building your goals, setting your goals, and gathering the tools to have your goals come true. Each time we set a goal and reach it, we have, in a sense, built a castle. Each time we build a castle, we have reached a goal that we set. With castle-building, there are many goals that must be reached along the way.

WRIGHT

Everything within these five steps are inner directed aren't they?

MICHELS

They are—they all focus on who we are inside and who we want to bring to the outside. The five steps help us to bring out what we want the outside to support who we are inside so that we can support more on the outside, then more of what we want will happen. What we want is who we are and who we are is what we really want. As we are more true to ourselves, the castles we envision will become our mission and these we will build for us and for others to stand up on.

WRIGHT

Makes good sense.

Well, what a great conversation. I really appreciate all this time you've taken to answer these questions. This castle-building concept sounds like a pretty good way to add to goal-setting. With so much introspection going on, it sounds like it might be hard at times, but it also sounds like it would be really worthwhile.

MICHELS

When you follow the five steps and you have that natural attitude of gratitude, it's easy to reach your goals. Castles are not built by individuals, they are built by communities. We are not doing any of this alone, no castle was every built by one person, all castles are built by and for the community. When we recognize that, and recognize that the commitment we make to ourselves is a commitment we make to the community, the world, and the universe. Then the community will make a commitment to support us. We will then not only get what we want, we will give what we have to give.

WRIGHT

Well, I really do appreciate the time you've taken with me this afternoon to answer these questions. You've given me a lot to think about and I know you have given our readers a lot to think about. I'm glad you are a part of this project.

MICHELS

I appreciate being in this project as well. I want to support others in reaching their goals, building their castles, and having miracles happen every day.

WRIGHT

Today we've been talking with Kate Michels. Kate is a veteran practitioner, trainer, and instructor in the field of self-help and life coaching. She is a sought-after motivational speaker and a best-selling author.

Kate, thank you so much for being with us today on *GPS to Success: Goals and Proven Strategies.*

MICHELS

Thank you.

ABOUT THE AUTHOR

Kate Michels is a popular, renowned, and established veteran practitioner, trainer, and instructor in the field of self-help and life coaching. Personally and professionally committed to life-freeing tools since being introduced to some of the great masters of the movement in high school, such as Milton Erickson, her commitment to everyone living up to their full potential reaches from pregnant women and their newborn infants to those who have committed crimes and are serving time in prison.

Creator, designer, facilitator, and chief instructor of Core Alignment Coaching, she is a best-selling author in several books. She is a sought-out motivational speaker, a "Wake Up Woman," Representative of the Summer of Peace, Center Point's LPIP Answer Woman, an "amazing dreamer," and a successful Real Estate broker in Portland, Oregon. Kate is also a wife, mother, daughter, sister, and grandmother. Her commitment to the principle that everyone is whole, perfect, creative, resourceful, and making the best decisions with the information they currently have, leads to her continued pursuit of gathering information. She has experienced lasting results with everything from bi-polar, anxiety issues, eating disorders, sleep issues, and just the normal struggles of everyday living.

Kate Michels

www.CoreAlignmentCoaching.com
CastleBuildingCoaching@yahoo.com

CHAPTER TEN

Square Bubbles and the Art of Wonder

An interview with...

Geoff Akins

DAVID WRIGHT (WRIGHT)

Today we're talking with Geoff Akins. Geoff has been entertaining and educating children for more than thirty years. His life-altering experience as a teacher in Waldorf and special education inspired him to create *The Bubble Wonders Show*. Performing more than three hundred times a year, he travels the world over as a speaker, author, and "edu-tainer." Geoff has been called a "modern day Johnny Appleseed, spreading his message far and wide, only working with bubbles instead of apple seeds, and children's souls instead of earth." His love of teaching and performing, combined with his gentle nature and gift of rapport with children, form a personal philosophy he calls "The Art of Wonder."

Geoff, welcome to *GPS for Success*.

GEOFF AKINS (AKINS)

Thank you, David; it's an honor to be here.

WRIGHT

So is it true that you make your living blowing bubbles?

AKINS

Yes, as strange as that may seem, I do indeed make a living playing with bubbles.

WRIGHT

That's great. So how did you get started in such an unusual career?

AKINS

It all started back when I was working as a teacher's assistant in a summer school program for preschoolers with special needs. I was moved by one of the students (a young boy with autism) who came in every day and left every day without interacting with the other kids or the staff. This was my first encounter with autism and my heart went out to this boy.

One day, I was off in the corner of the room looking through some puzzles and games when I found a bottle of bubbles. I was captivated because I hadn't played with bubbles since I was a little kid. My curiosity got the better of me and soon I was blowing bubbles for my own amusement.

After a moment or two I sensed someone next to me and I turned and here was this young autistic boy. He had stopped whatever activity he had been immersed in to come over to see what I was doing with the bubbles.

I was amazed that this child was seeking any sort of interaction with me. I looked up to see the teacher taking all this in from across the room. She silently mouthed the words, "Oh, My, God!" I mimed back, "What do I do?" Neither of us had a clue so I just kept blowing bubbles for as long as the boy was engaged, thankful for the connection.

For a long time afterward, all I did was wonder, "What else could I have done with the bubbles to lengthen that period of time he allowed me into his world?" I didn't know it at the moment, but asking that question planted a seed that has since blossomed into a calling.

WRIGHT

That sounds wonderful, but I have to ask this, can you truly earn enough to support yourself simply by playing with bubbles? Has the economy effected what you do?

AKINS

That's a great question. Often, when I tell somebody I'm a professional "bubbleologist," they laugh at me and say, "No, seriously, what's your *real* job? What do you do for a living?" I have to explain to them this *is* my real job and I never feel *more* real than when I'm motivating both children and adults using nothing more than common ordinary soap bubbles.

Am I able to support myself? Yes! In fact, in March I set a new personal record when I earned in a month what I once made in a year at my previous job.

WRIGHT

Well, the economy sure hasn't affected you at all then, has it?

AKINS

Not at all, David. In fact, I'm actually turning down certain opportunities and referring those clients to other entertainers I know and trust. This is a wonderful win-win situation—the clients receive quality entertainment, my performing colleagues (some of whom *have* been hit hard by the economy) receive some much needed work, and it allows me the opportunity to focus on the types of clients I can best serve, as my emphasis shifts more toward my writing and speaking services.

WRIGHT

So you mentioned children *and* adults. Is this meant more for children or for adults? Who is your target audience?

AKINS

It depends on the client. On average, I speak/perform three hundred times a year. Some are presentations for schools, libraries, businesses, daycare and senior centers, churches, museums, etc. Those are primarily children and family events.

On the other hand, I'm also hired for a variety of speaking engagements presenting keynotes and breakout sessions at conferences on education, health and wellness, creativity, hospice, personal development, and improving the life of seniors. I've done everything from opening for the indie rock duo Mates of State live in concert to creating bubbles for an IBM advertisement! The core message I offer is so universal it appeals to a wide variety of clientele. What I do speaks to both the child and to the child inside the adult.

WRIGHT

I'm sure you've given it a lot of thought, but would you tell our readers why you think your show is so successful?

AKINS

I believe it's successful for a number of reasons. First, there's the curiosity factor. What I do is so unusual that people are drawn to it because of the novelty. We've all seen your typical magicians and jugglers and clowns before. It's old news. Likewise, people in the business world have heard the same sort of keynote speeches over and over again, too. So when something new comes along, we're captivated by it. A booking agent at one of the speaker's bureaus recently told me he likes what I do because most speakers are informative but rather dry because their presentations are so data-laden. He calls what I do "a breath of fresh air" and people respond to that in a positive way.

But novelty alone is not enough. You might momentarily capture someone's attention with some new way of presenting your ideas but it must be followed with substance and heart, otherwise it just becomes another gimmick. A very perceptive woman realized this after a recent presentation and remarked with a knowing smile, "It's not about the bubbles at all, is it?" She understood! It's *not* about the bubbles. I'm merely using bubbles as a way to capture and focus the attention of the audience, to create a sense of wonder and possibility, illustrating my points in a visually enchanting way. Once the audience is open and receptive, all the positive messages about making dreams come true find fertile ground in their imagination.

Interacting with the audience in this way is extremely effective. It forms a powerful connection, a wonderful rapport. Many clients have commented on the gentle way in which I interact with children. More than once I've been called either the Willy Wonka of Bubbles or the Mr. Rogers of Bubbles!

I believe this way of presenting (I call it "the art of wonder") stirs something in adults, too. In fact, the main reason we're even having this conversation is because Wendy from your Insight Publishing office happened to catch my performance during a television interview and relentlessly tracked me down with multiple phone calls, e-mails, and messages on Facebook because she was so captivated by the experience. When we finally connected, the first thing she said was, "I've never seen a speaker quite like you before. Your enthusiasm just shines through and what you do is so unique we just have to share your story with our readers!"

WRIGHT

So what are the core themes or messages in your show?

AKINS

The core theme of *The Bubble Wonders Show* is "anything is possible!" In order to prove that statement is true, I attempt to create a seemingly impossible object—a square bubble. Along the way, I intentionally fail a time or two in order to model persistence—

sharing how just because something is possible doesn't necessarily mean it's going to be easy to accomplish. So if we have a dream and a worthwhile goal, we have to keep trying even if the going gets tough.

Another related theme is all about the power of our beliefs. I share how it doesn't matter how old we are or how tall or small we are or what's happened in our past, what matters is what we choose to believe now. If we believe we can accomplish something, then we're more likely to achieve our goals. What matters most is following your heart and persevering with a positive attitude.

WRIGHT

So what sort of response have you received? Would you share some examples?

AKINS

Sure, I have files full of positive feedback and I post some of it on my Web site (BubbleShows.com) and in my e-mail newsletters, too. Here are a few of my personal favorites. The first comes from a camp director in Chicago:

"In today's world of empty entertainment, your show was a welcome change. Your performance had such depth and meaning. Your personal quest to create a square bubble, and persistence in accomplishing that goal, gave our students great food for thought. Your message of 'anything is possible' resonated through the entire performance. It is our fervent hope that your powerful message and charming presentation reaches and affects many more children"

—*Rivkie K.*

Here's a letter that touched my heart:

"I wanted to extend a lesson I learned while watching your show here in our small town of Bluffton, Indiana. It was mentioned to you before the show that my husband and I actually postponed our vacation an entire week because our three-and-a-half-year-old daughter had been waiting all summer long to see your program.

"Every day she asked, 'Can I see the Bubble Man today?' At long last we donned our traveling clothes and went to see your long-awaited performance. Very rarely have I seen our daughter so engaged and managed to sit so still. Thank you for allowing her to have the special privilege of being inside the bubble at the end of the show. Seeing the excitement and the thrill and the wonder on Bella's face that morning made me glad we waited to leave for vacation.

"Something else tells me it was even God-sent. You see, the day prior I learned my teaching position of four years had been cut due to budget increases. I was crushed, wondering who or what I would be if I didn't have my classroom. Many emotions ensued that day and continued into the next. Little did I know that God can use bubbles to minister to a broken heart; your message of 'anything is possible' kept ringing in my mind.

"Obviously, something would have to be possible for me, but what? So I kept watching with increased anticipation to see this impossible square bubble you promised because my life was quickly leading into a square bubble of its own.

"Along with the rest of the crowd, my eyes widened and my jaw dropped when the impossible finally made itself known, with the support from the other bubbles around it, a square bubble was possible. Without that support, the square bubble would pop.

"As I begin this new journey in my life, whether it be for a year or the beginning of a new lifetime, I know anything is possible because I have the support of so many others and allow myself to be pushed into shape by the One who made me. Thank you for ministering to kids of all ages, especially me!"

—*Nikkei Bradley.*

Those are just a couple of examples of why the response to Bubble Wonders is so overwhelmingly positive. I will share some other examples throughout the interview. You know you're doing something right when parents rearrange their travel plans so their children can attend *The Bubble Wonders Show!*

WRIGHT

Wow, what a powerful affirmation. Well, those are nice to get aren't they? So you actually *do* make a square bubble?

AKINS

Yes!

WRIGHT

Oh my, I'd travel to see that.

AKINS

I would love to have you come to a performance. You can also visit BubbleShows.com and check out the videos and photographs, too!

WRIGHT

Do you advertise or promote your services?

AKINS

Early on I advertised heavily to schools and libraries but not so much anymore. Now it's primarily word-of-mouth referrals and repeat clients. A large percentage of my clients book me year after year. Time and time again I hear, "That was the best program we've ever had!" Museums and libraries love *The Bubble Wonders Show* because it consistently brings in a record-setting number of patrons. People talk about the show and it just spreads like wildfire. Every time I perform at schools, principals and teachers and PTA staff tell their colleagues at other schools. The same holds true for daycare centers, libraries, camps, scouts—you name it. Each television appearance I make results in a surge in new clients as well.

This past February I presented the keynote at the Changing the World One Child at a Time conference in West Virginia. The response was amazing! And who do you think attends these conferences? Teachers, principals, librarians, daycare directors, etc. do. All of these people are constantly looking for quality programs for their children and staff. I hear it all the time, "I just know all my kids back home will love this!" It's the ripple effect in action.

WRIGHT

Do you have any advice for others who are on a similar path?

AKINS

I do, and some of it is really simple. A fellow performer recently said, "You work more than 95 percent of the performers I know. What's your secret?" Even people outside of my profession are beginning to notice the results I've achieved. Earlier this week I received e-mails from two different local businessmen asking, "How do you get on television?" and "How do you get all these wonderful articles written about you?" Here are some of the ideas that have worked for me:

Be Different: do something so unique that it somehow sets you apart from the crowd. Working with bubbles did that for me. From the very beginning, all my promotional materials posed the same question in bold letters at the top of the page: "Looking for something *new* and *different*? Look No Further!" I appealed to people's innate curiosity: "Aren't we all looking for something new and different?" I hoped the question would capture their attention long enough to read the rest of my copy—and it worked! If you're trying to get media attention, offer something so different and so "juicy" that they have no choice but to notice you.

When I first started out, I contacted all the local television news programs in early March and offered to make myself completely available to come on the show and create a square bubble anytime during the first week of spring. I explained how this would be a great tie-in since it's also National Bubbles Week. Then I offered to attempt to break the world record for the longest chain of bubbles live on air during the broadcast. Finally, I offered to put one of the reporters *inside* a bubble! Do you think they took me up on the offer? Of course they did! It was just too good to pass up! And they've invited me back repeatedly. The same ripple effect I mentioned with conferences and schools and libraries holds true for newspapers and television, too. Soon offers were coming in from all the other major networks.

"What really impressed me was how Geoff's level of experience in dealing with children was clearly obvious throughout the show. He anticipated every time the kids' enthusiasm could have gotten out of hand, either because of humor (Geoff is very funny) or because of the 'wow-factor' (Geoff's bubble tricks are amazing), and quickly brought the group right back under control. Geoff kept the students quiet and respectful while at the same time having a ton of fun"—*Heidi Schmuldt, Park View Elementary School.*

Exceed Expectations: This is another guiding idea in my business. So many people who hire me do so with an expectation of receiving an educational program they hope will hold the children's attention for a little while. If the show is also entertaining, they feel it's icing on the cake. But rarely are they prepared for the depth of the messages and how engaged the children and the adults are throughout the show.

"The audience was enthralled with your performance. The bubble manipulation was wonderful, but what I never expected was your subtle, but ever present positive message— 'anything is possible.' While I remembered the general meaning of your message, our six-year-old granddaughter repeated it verbatim on the way home! I was quite surprised. When we talked about it again on Wednesday, she still remembered your exact words! Even more impressive!"— *Linda Menart.*

People come up to me and hug me after the show saying this was just what they needed to hear because things had somehow gone wrong in their own life. They needed that validation and inspiration to get back out there. Essentially, what we're talking about is hope.

Then there are the little personal touches. After the show, I might stay and perform an extra bubble trick or two for the client's children. I might give them a bubble wand or even offer to put them inside a bubble for photographs. Another little ritual I love is when I allow the boys and girls (and an adventurous adult or two) to come up after the show to share their dream while touching a special "magic bubble" that I've turned into a solid ball during the performance. I also give away copies of my books to each of my clients as my way of saying thanks.

Do The Right Thing: Personal integrity and doing the right thing are also important. Keeping your word is crucial. I was once hired to give the service at a church in Louisville, Kentucky. The city was hit by a major ice storm right before the show. President Obama declared it a national disaster, yet I honored my word and made the trip. While I was there, I met a few new friends who helped me spontaneously coordinate an impromptu performance at the temporary shelter set up by the Red Cross to house those who had lost power in the storm and were forced out of their homes.

"Thank you for living your message, 'anything is possible.' The adults shared how much they appreciated your Sunday presentation and how they enjoyed hearing the children's laughter in the church service. Standing ovations are rare—your spirit touched people's lives. And weren't you just blown away when a four-year-old child walked up to you after the service to say, 'Thank you, Mr. Bubbleman, I'm soooo happy you're here!' Loving blessings."

—Rev. Susan EngPoole

Now that was an extreme case. Other times it's something much less dramatic. If you're an entertainer (or in any line of business) even the smallest things can make a big difference.

WRIGHT

Will you give us an example?

AKINS

Sure! One time, on tour in Texas, I needed an extra table for my show and one of the custodians helped me carry it over to the stage. After the show, I was putting all my things away and I moved the table back to where it belonged; the two custodians exchanged open-mouthed looks at each other. Concerned, I asked them what was wrong and they replied, "You're the first presenter we've ever had who put the table back where it belongs after the show rather than leave it for us to do!"

Again, it was such a simple thing. But they add up and here's the bottom line: as budget cuts make clients more selective about who they're going to hire, I want to be the one who stands out in their memory as a class act! It's been said that people may not remember what you say or what you do but they always remember how you made them feel. My goal is three out of three! What did he *say*? "Anything is possible!" What did he *do*? He made a square bubble! How did he make me *feel*? Entertained, uplifted and inspired!

Do What You Love: If you're passionate about what you do, that passion and enthusiasm shines through and people respond to your energy and excitement. People love a good story. If you have a story about why you do what you do, then make sure to share that with others, too. You never know who you might inspire! Countless people have asked me after a presentation how I first started in this whole bubble business. When I tell them about my encounter with the little autistic boy, the presentation suddenly becomes meaningful on a much deeper level. I believe sharing my own "back story" is one of the reasons the show is so popular.

WRIGHT

I think I might have figured out how I can blow a square bubble. I'll take a straw and blow it into a little square box and freeze it.

AKINS

That's a great idea, David! See, even though we've continued our conversation, your curiosity is *still* working over the question of how to make a square bubble. I love that! You've just experienced a little of what my audiences experience during *The Bubble Wonders Show.*

WRIGHT

So who inspired you? Did you have any mentors when you started out and now?

AKINS

I do. First I'd like to mention my bubble mentor, Tom Noddy. Tom is the one who introduced bubble magic to the world in the early 1980s. Most of the things I do with these delicate orbs of soap and water (including the square bubble) are tricks Tom either invented or refined over the last forty years of his performance career. I lovingly refer to him as my "Bubble Godfather."

Next, would be magician Doug Henning. I remember seeing all of Doug's television specials as a child and his gentle stage presence has certainly influenced my own style of performing.

Some of my mentors are authors I love.

I am a huge Wayne Dyer fan. His book, *Manifest Your Destiny,* changed my life in profound ways. I also love Richard Bach, Deepak Chopra, Carlos Castaneda, and many others. I'm also inspired by a small handful of amazing singer-songwriters including Greg Tamblyn, Jana Stanfield, and Martin Sexton. Just add dot com to any of their names to visit them online!

Inspiration can also come in the form of quotes that have touched my life. Earlier today my sister-in-law shared the following with me:

"'To laugh often and much; to win the respect of intelligent people and the affection of children . . . to leave the world a better place . . . to know even one life has breathed easier because you have lived. This is to have succeeded'—Ralph Waldo Emerson.

"I saw this quote and immediately thought of you. I don't know anyone else who has not only reached all these goals, but continues to do so each and every day. You're an inspiration to us all!" (Janet Akins).

One of my personal favorites quotes is, "Ask not what the world needs, ask what makes you come alive and then go do it, because what this world needs is people who have come alive"—*Howard Thurman.*

Carlos Castaneda called it "finding a path with heart." Speaking of this, on my GPS there is a setting for my favorite destinations. The icon for the setting is a heart. I love that! I believe it's true of our own inner GPS too. If we touch or connect with the heart, we automatically set a course to our ultimate destination! I whole*heartedly* embrace the "Do What You Love" and "Follow Your Bliss" philosophy. I've heard and loved those quotes for years but it took me awhile to actually embrace it personally and live it as a truth!

Now I share what I've learned during my presentations. Inevitably, there comes a moment in the show where the audience and I are laughing and I stop and ask, "Can you tell I love my job?" They smile and nod. I tell them that when I was a boy, someone told me, "Do what you love and you'll never work a day in your life." It took me more than forty years to finally *act* on that bit of wisdom. Now, I'm trying to help shorten the learning curve for others by using my own story as an example. Of course, the truth is I *do* still have to work. In fact, I've never worked longer and harder in my life; but it's work I love and that makes all the difference in the world!

WRIGHT

So what's next for Geoff Akins?

AKINS

Professionally, there are lots of great things up ahead. I'm working on a series of videos and workshops to teach others how to achieve their dreams, and I have several book projects in various stages of development too. On a deeper, more personal level, I've realized the importance of one final step or idea I'd like to share with you.

Giving Back in Joyful Service: When I was a younger man, the thought of service always made me feel anxious because I thought it meant working in a soup kitchen when I felt my life was more about making children happy. Then one day I came across the following quote:

"I slept and dreamt that life was joy; I awoke and found that life was service; I acted and behold service was joy!"

—Rabindranath Tagore.

It was such an epiphany when I realized my love of performing *is* the best way for me to serve—it's joyful service! I tested out this new-found theory in November of 2009 when I gave back in the form of a "volun-tourism" trip with singer-songwriter, Jana Stanfield. We traveled to Singapore and Bali where I performed my Bubble Wonders show and shared the "anything is possible" message of hope with all the boys and girls in various orphanages we visited there. It was an amazing experience! The highlight for me was meeting Sari, the orphan girl I've been sponsoring for the last couple of years. (A $400 donation to BaliFund.org provides a child with schooling and room and board for an entire year!) This year a group of us will be serving in Thailand, Cambodia, and Vietnam.

Lately, I've been stepping out of my comfort zone in a new direction that has me feeling both excited and a little anxious. But that's a good thing! Someone once said that if your goals aren't making you feel a little bit uncomfortable, then chances are they're probably not ambitious enough. Joseph Campbell said, "The cave you fear to enter holds the treasure that you seek."

WRIGHT

Will you tell our readers what's inside this particular cave?

AKINS

Sure. As I've mentioned, children are a constant source of inspiration and act as touchstones in my life. It was a child who first guided me into this magical, life-changing world of bubbles. It was another child who inspired me to take a leap of faith and leave teaching to pursue my performing and speaking full-time. I share those amazing experiences in more detail in my latest book, *Empowered*.

Most recently, it was another child who has inspired me to move in a new direction. A while back, I attended a Celebrate Your Life conference featuring inspirational speakers like Wayne Dyer, Deepak Chopra, Maryanne Williamson, and Neil Donald Walsh. At a lunch break, I was sitting next to a grandmother and her eight-year-old granddaughter. I thought it was wonderful that this woman was giving her grandchild a chance to hear all these life-changing ideas.

At one point during our conversation, this woman asked me what I do for a living. I told her all about *The Bubble Wonders Show* and its message of anything is possible. Finding her receptive and supportive, I confessed something I hadn't yet shared with anyone else up to that point: "I keep feeling like I'm being guided to do more work with children who are sick or dying." It was at that point her granddaughter joined the conversation for the first time.

"I can *see* it—" she began, nodding her head. Her grandmother gently nudged me without taking her eyes off the girl whispering, "Listen to her—she *knows* things."

I faced the girl and asked, "What do you mean?"

The girl turned and met my gaze and continued, "When you mentioned working with children who are sick or dying I saw an image of you as an older man in your sixties and seventies and these young men and women in their twenties and thirties coming up to you saying 'I saw your show when I was very sick in the hospital as a child and that message of anything is possible is the reason I'm still here.' "

I got goosebumps just now telling you about it! What a powerful message—and to hear it from a child! I can't begin to describe how her words have totally transformed the way I view what I do. Since then, I have had several opportunities to donate performances at hospitals and fundraisers for a variety of causes.

This past April Fool's Day I joined the Association of Applied and Therapeutic Humor. This coming April I'll have the honor of presenting the opening keynote address at the AATH's 24th Annual conference at Disney's Lake Buena Vista Palace in Orlando, Florida. My goal is to network with as many kindred spirits as possible in order to learn as much as I can about the effects of belief and prayer and laughter on healing. I feel there is so much potential in this area of research.

A nurse came up to me after one of these presentations and said, "You must remember this message of 'anything is possible' takes on a much deeper meaning in the kinds of life-and-death-situations these children and their families are facing." And she's absolutely right! If anything truly is possible then those possibilities are limitless!

My greatest hope is planting the seeds of possibility when people are at their most vulnerable can perhaps inspire their will to live and lead them toward healing and recovery. If that's not their destiny, then at the very least, I hope it can help them come to some sense of closure and acceptance of their situation. In preparation for the latter eventuality, I've taken training as both a hospice volunteer and as a volunteer with the Make a Wish Foundation. If it *is* a child's time to go I want to help make the time remaining as memorable as possible. And I want to shake awake the rest of us and say, "Let's not wait until we're on our deathbed in the hope that others will make our dreams come true!"

When all is said and done, I'm fully aware that how the message of "anything is possible" affects others is ultimately out of my hands; but I do see it as my personal responsibility and life's work to share that message of perpetual hope and optimism for as long as I possibly can.

WRIGHT

Well, I hope you're able to share that message for many years to come.

Geoff, I really appreciate all the time you've spent with me here answering these questions. What you do is fascinating and I wish you continued success.

AKINS

Thank you.

WRIGHT

Today we've been talking with Geoff Akins. He has been entertaining and educating children for more than thirty years. His life-altering experiences, as related here today, inspired him to create *The Bubble Wonders Show*. I can't wait to see it myself. His love of teaching and performing, combined with his gentle nature and gift of rapport with children, form a personal philosophy he calls "the art of wonder."

Geoff, thank you so much for being with us today on *GPS for Success*.

AKINS

Thanks for having me, David. It was an honor.

About the Author

Geoff Akins travels the world as an author, speaker, and performer. Geoff has presented in China, Mexico, Bali, Hong Kong, Singapore, Israel, and Vietnam. Here at home in the United States, he has been featured on ABC, NBC and *CBS Sunday Morning* with Charles Osgood.

Akins is a member of the National Speakers Association, the International Speakers Network, the Society of American Magicians, the American Library Association, and the Association of Applied and Therapeutic Humor. His clients include IBM, Macy's, Whole Foods, Gymboree, Allstate, Toyota, and the National Geographic Channel.

Geoff is the co-author of the self-improvement number one best-seller, *Empowered!* Akins donates a portion of all proceeds of the sale of his books to Autism Speaks, the American Cancer Society, and the Make a Wish Foundation.

Geoff Akins
The Art of Wonder LLC
Barrington, IL
847-668-2808
info@BubbleShows.com
www.BubbleShows.com

CHAPTER ELEVEN
Start Where You Stand: Finding Life Balance

An interview with...

Sallie Felton

DAVID WRIGHT (WRIGHT)

Today we're talking with Sallie Felton. Sallie is living proof that people can go through a major life change and not only survive but thrive. After years of frustration and searching for her purpose she decided to leave her proper Yankee upbringing, traditional education and competitive sports career to pursue her true passions. It's been twenty years and she hasn't looked back. Now she is helping others do the same.

Sallie is a fully certified CMC, PCC life coach, transition specialist, international talk radio host, author, and motivational speaker. When working with her clients, she uses their individual strengths to create and support their successful life goals. Through one-on-one, as well as group coaching, she has helped thousands. She says to her clients, "Start where you stand."

Sallie Felton, welcome to *GPS for Success: Goals and Proven Strategies*.

FELTON

David, thank you for asking me to contribute to this wonderful book, I am truly honored.

WRIGHT

So tell me, you and I have heard many, many definitions of life balance. How do you define life balance?

FELTON

It's interesting that you bring this up. I was curious what Webster's Dictionary would say about defining the word *life* so I looked it up. And I quote, "The quality that distinguishes a vital and functional plant or animal from a dead body; or a state of living characterized by capacity for metabolism, or growth, or reaction to stimulus or reproduction." That's what they say about the definition of life. It sounds so dry to me.

Balance is another word we try to find in our work/life existence. Webster says, "An instrument for weighing a being that is supported freely in the center and has two pans of equal weight suspended from its end . . ."

When I think of putting those two words together I think of life balance similar to the growth of a tree. Metaphorically, if you were to think of a tree, it's being nourished, it's always growing, it's always blossoming, and sometimes it's being pruned by nature with earnest. If on one side of that tree, David, it becomes too laden with branches, what happens? It loses its balance and it leans to one side or another. Just as in life, if we become too overworked we become laden with stress, so we become *out* of balance.

> *"There is just one life for each of us, our own."*
> —Euripides

I think that is so true and I believe in it whole heartedly. When do we get to live our life again? For our life is *not* a dress rehearsal—this is it! So in order to be the very best we can be, we need to honor and be responsible for our own life—not the lives of others around us, we are responsible and accountable for *our own*. Period!

Each of us needs to create balance if we are feeling "out on a limb," but how do we make it? I always say, "By starting and standing just where you are."

During my childhood, a very wise, dear lady, Hazel Young, used to say, "Start where you stand." Just by being present we begin to ask the questions: what is our balance, where do we go, how do we get there? Today, more than ever in our world, we see people stressed to the max and looking for balance. Why are they stressed? What's made them so? Here are a couple of things that account for this:

- Working to support a lifestyle they have become accustomed to
- Fearing job security, especially in these economic times
- Being the only caregiver/single parent attributes to even more stress
- Caring for their elderly parents as well as their own families
- Maintaining their own houses or apartments
- Finding time for spirituality
- Finding time for each other
- Trying to keep a healthy body
- Being part of the community and giving back

So how in the world can they stay balanced?

WRIGHT

No wonder people are so frazzled.

You use a metaphor of the tree of life to depict life balance. Will you explain to our reader why that is important?

FELTON

I love this metaphor. First, picture a tree in your mind. It sits there high on a hill, tall and majestic. Its roots go deep into the earth, getting nourishment from the water well below the surface of the earth. Now think of the trunk of the tree symbolizing *life balance*. From the trunk grows the branches—many, many branches—all different in length and size. Let's now name *each* of the different branches with these categories:

❖ PROFESSION/JOB ❖ FINANCE

❖ PHYSICAL ❖ HEALTH

❖ SPIRITUAL ❖ SOCIAL SUPPORT

❖ INTIMACY ❖ FAMILY

❖ LEARNING/GROWING ❖ HOME

❖ OFFICE ❖ ENVIRONMENT

❖ PLAY ❖ FUN

So you can see that this tree is pretty full. Now I ask you, "is this tree blooming?" Look closely at the tree that you have envisioned. Is there any part that needs to be pruned? One can easily realize that some work might need to be done on each of the branches in order for it to be in full bloom or blossoming. Now the million-dollar question always is, "how is this done?" This could be a daunting process for many, many people.

Here is a way to gauge where we have or don't have life balance in our lives just by using the model of each of the tree branches. Now that you have labeled *each* of the branches, you will now give it an amount or a value. In order to do this, label it zero to ten, with ten being you are the most confident or happy with the way your life is balanced. Place an amount/value for each of the branches of your life. For example, if you were looking at the branch labeled finance, and you were to put a value of four on that branch, this would be the common dialogue:

Sallie: "What does four represent for you—what makes it a four?"

Client: "With four I am somewhat on the low side of being fulfilled with my finance"

Sallie: "What would make it a four and a half?"

Client: "Well I'm not sure."

Sallie: "If you did know, what would you need to do to make it a four and a half?"

Here's where the balance comes into play. When you move forward with one thing—by moving that four to a four and a half—something on the other branches has to give way or adjust. Something has to be pruned back, you can't be adding to this tree because it's going to be over-laden. You have to make choices.

When I go back to the client, the conversation could sound something like this:

Sallie: "All right, looking at your finances, how could you move that forward? What would you need to do?"

Client: "Well, I could be more productive at work and do less of X, Y, and Z [whatever that is]."

Sallie: "What does that bring you?"

Client: "I could get more work done than I am presently doing."

Sallie: "And if you have more productivity, what does that give you?"

Client: "I would be recognized for the job that I am doing and feel more valued."

Sallie: "And then what?"

Client: "I might be highlighted/noticed when it comes to a performance review."

Sallie: "And why is that important?"

Client: "It could give me a raise."

So we do that throughout all of those fourteen categories, putting a value from zero to ten on each one. What we're trying to do is to see what is lopsided, what direction it is leaning, and where we are feeling over-laden in all areas of our life.

People have to see their whole life in order to see where they *need* balance. One does not have to have straight fives or sevens in their life to create total balance. There could be different degrees as they begin the process of balancing their life. David, it seems so simple, but this is where people get stuck. They don't take the time to sit down and see where their life could be more balanced and what they could do to take just one step forward.

By being *in* balance means we're feeding our soul with something we love to do and we're also taking care of that which we're not so fond of doing.

WRIGHT

What happens if someone feels satisfied with all aspects, but still feels no balance?

FELTON

Good question and I've seen that many, many times. Here is the next step to consider. With each of the branches, I have my clients dissect how they use their time on another sheet of paper.

For example, the conversation might go like this:

Sallie: "Tell me, how do you spend your time? Look at your whole day. If you're not completing what you need to accomplish during that day, let's look at that. What are you doing hourly? How many hours do you want to work in a day? How many hours do you want to work to feel balanced?"

Client: "Well, I want to work ten hours or maybe work eight."

Sallie: "Great! That's awesome. Which is it? How are you going to make that happen? What does this look like for you?"

Client: "I want to work eight hours, though I don't know—it just gets so busy; the time just gets away from me. I'm feeling stressed, I'm not feeling balanced."

Sallie: "Well let's look at your day. What time do you start your day? Tell me what you do."

So we literally go through every single hour of the day. By doing that with my clients, we find out:

- If they have wasted time
- Where they have wasted time
- If they haven't wasted time
- Where they are most productive
- What time of the day are they most energized
- When people feel alive, they are their best

Would they not be better served by using their more alive energy time when they're really awake for some of those more difficult tasks in their jobs, rather than leaving that toward the end of the day when they feel dragged down? And why? Makes sense doesn't it?

Thus, little by little, we start to make a shift in their day, so they're feeling more balanced with what they're doing. Then we look at the whole week. They ask themselves where are they finding time for:

- Family during the day during the week
- Spirituality
- Physical Needs
- Learning
- Play
- Fun
- Social Support, and so forth

When shifts are made, something must be added/rearranged and something must be let go. All of that is very, very important.

"The difficulty lays not so much in developing new ideas as in escaping from the old ones."
—John Maynard Keynes

WRIGHT

So you say to bring balance to someone's life there must be a letting go. Will you explain that to us?

FELTON

Yes, exactly—there does need to be a letting go. In order to attract and receive balance, something has to be relinquished. As I said earlier, if you take on something in your life, something else needs to be removed. Otherwise, they would crumble under the weight of their stress.

For example, if the tree is too full, the wind will naturally prune it. In order to prune back what you have to do during your day, you have to say no to something, and if you are saying no to something, then what are you saying yes to? If people have too much on their plate and they are feeling overburdened and stressed, something has to give in their life. It will happen, it has to. Just as the tree is nourished by the rain, the same holds true for people. When they are fed with a life of balance, they are fueled both physically and spiritually. It's important for us to do that; it's really important for us to start to begin to say no. So it is all about the choice once again. How important is life balance to people?

WRIGHT

I've heard you say before in some of your radio shows, *A Fresh Start with Sallie Felton,* that it's important to say "no" in your life. You say too many people don't do that, which only brings on more stress to fulfill someone else's needs. So how does one overcome that and begin to use "no" to balance their life?

FELTON

That's a great question, David. Let me use this example: It's a Saturday afternoon and you have a document or project for the office due on Monday, but your child also has a soccer game that same afternoon. Which do you do? *What are your priorities?* If you very much want to go to your child's soccer game, you would be more apt to say yes to attend the soccer game for a couple of reasons: 1) you don't want to disappoint your child by not being there, 2) you like the interaction with the other parents. *But* what about that project? You have a deadline and it *must* be done by Monday. This is where choices and time management come into play. So is there a way, without saying no to your child, that you can say yes, *but* say no to some invitation you know will come along by talking with one of the parents on the sidelines? Can you do that without feeling guilty or feeling as if you have let someone down? This is the important piece is saying *no*. If you were to participate with the other parents after the game, you are using that time instead of working on the office project. This is where people get into trouble—*they try to do it all.*

Here again, it's making good choices—choices of balance that's important. It's crucial we don't keep saying yes to friends or commitments for more time when we need to be saying *no* in order to simplify their life. It's important we don't dilly-dally, procrastinate, or while the time away. Then, when time is of the essence, we won't stress.

"Our lives are fritted away in detail . . . simplify, simplify, simplify, I believe with simplicity, balance occurs"
—Henry David Thoreau

If we can balance the branches of our own lives, we will be a fully mature tree. How much more special that can be—in full bloom, without cracks, without bruises, without disease? We will have balanced ourselves. But in order to do that, *each branch needs to be taken care of,* not just one, but the entire array of branches; it's so important.

WRIGHT

So would you be willing to share an example from your own experience when you felt out of balance and what you did to solve that?

FELTON

Absolutely. I was in my mid thirties, married with three children—ages five, three, and a newborn. I was the owner and manufacturer of a small business called The Rocking Horse. We manufactured children's small vests, outwear, jackets, and clothing from toddlers to a child's size ten. I would go to Boston to buy the fabric, meet with my sales reps throughout New England, design eight to twelve appliqués for the vests and jackets, send off the pieces to be sewed to my seamstresses, send the garments to different stores nationwide, do all the invoicing and billing, and on top of all that I was going to expositions! My business was a cottage industry.

At this time, David, I wanted to be a "stay-at-home mom," but didn't want to give up the business. I felt stretched and I didn't have enough hours during the day. I was coming to the workshop exhausted because I would set my alarm clock for 2 AM, start working and nurse my newborn all at the same time. I felt depleted and everyone was feeling it.

During one 2 AM stretch, my husband came to me and said, "Sallie, I know you love to do this, I know you do, and I would never say you couldn't do it, but would you at least consider putting this on hold? You're exhausted, are you really having fun at this anymore?"

That was a major ah-ha! moment for me, David! By having someone else say that to me and not say you have to sell my business or give it up, but to put it on hold was a kinder, gentler way of saying, "Where is your life balance?" That made all the difference. And I did—I did put it on hold. And it wasn't so much a process of getting rid of it, but knowing I could always bring it back if I wanted to (even in a different form). So I did and again, it was *by letting go of something* that allowed me to be with my children. I was clearly feeling out of balance. That for me was a turning point. That's where I began to say "no," instead of taking on more.

> *"If there is no struggle, there is no progress."*
> —Frederick Douglas

WRIGHT

So how do you keep a full-time life coaching business, being an international talk radio host, an avid outdoor person, a lover of gardens, wife, and mother of three adult children, all of them extreme athletes? How do you keep it together?

FELTON

I sat down and I asked myself, "What are your priorities, Sallie? What do you want to do? What don't you want to do?" I thought about a lot of things. I thought long and hard. I actually made a list. Some people make a vision board or list goals. Whatever works for you, do it. My family comes first, my life coaching is second, and my radio show is third. In order to make that happen, I had to simplify my life, one step at a time.

There are times now when my friends say, "Can you do X, Y, or Z?" If our adult children are home, I find myself wanting to be with them because they don't live close by—they live in Wyoming and Colorado. So I would say gracefully, "No," to their kind invitation. My usual reply would go something like this: "I would love to be with you, but our kids are home and I really want to be home with them." That was important for me to let go of the guilt with my friends. It is so hard because no one wants to disappoint anyone. If our friends didn't understand, David, it wasn't my job to make them understand. But in order for me to have a balanced life, that's what I needed to do, not only for *myself* but for my family.

Another thing is I needed to find time for myself. I either journal, I'm out digging in my garden early in the morning, or I walk with my dog. Something I have always done each day is to make it a habit of always looking for something new that I have not seen before. I might drive the same route as I run my errands, but I always look for something new along the way. That not only brings to me "seeing something new brightens my day," it's exciting to me, it also continues the curiosity that every day something is going to be new and different and no day is the same. *I love that!*

WRIGHT

You always ask your guests on your radio show to leave your listeners with a pearl. What is a pearl that you could leave with our readers here on *GPS to Success: Goals and Proven Strategies?*

FELTON

Sometimes I have guests who end with a quote and I think this is so appropriate for the topic of life balance. Well, here is something that I'd love to leave with our readers:

LOOK TO THIS DAY

Look to this day!
For it is life, the very life of life,
In its brief course lie all
Varieties and realities of your existence;
The bliss of growth,
The glory of action,
The splendor of beauty;
For yesterday is but a dream
And tomorrow is only a vision,
But today well lived makes
Every yesterday a dream of happiness,
And every tomorrow a vision of hope.
Look well, therefore, to this day!

—Kālidāsa, classical Sanskrit writer

WRIGHT

Well said. I really appreciate all this time you've taken with me today, Sallie, to answer these questions. Life balance is always an important topic and I think you have some unique views on this. I'm going to think about it and I'm sure our readers will enjoy this part of the book.

FELTON

Well, David, thank you, and I am again honored to be a part of this book and look forward to sharing many more thoughts with many of your readers.

WRIGHT

Today we've been talking with Sallie Felton. Sallie is a fully certified CMC, PCC life coach, a transition specialists, and co-author who uses her clients' individual strengths to create and support their successful life goals. Through one-on-one and group coaching, she helps her clients move forward at their pace one step at a time. And listening to her today, I think she knows what she's talking about, at least I believe it.

Sallie, thank you so much for being with us today on *GPS to Success: Goals and Proven Strategies*.

FELTON

David, thank you so much, and let's put the "L" back in the word *living*.

About the Author

Sallie Felton is living proof that people can go through a major life change and not only survive, but thrive. After years of frustration and searching for her purpose she decided to leave her proper Yankee upbringing, traditional education, and competitive sports career to pursue her true passions. It's been twenty years and she hasn't looked back. Now she is helping others do the same. Sallie is an international radio talk show host, fully certified CMC, PCC Life Coach, Transition Specialist, international talk radio host, author, and motivational speaker who uses her clients' individual strengths to create and support their life goals. Through one-on-one and group coaching she has helped thousands; as she says to her clients, "Start where you stand."

Sallie Felton
P.O. Box 264
Hamilton, MA 01936
978-626-0090
sallie@salliefeltonlifecoach.com
www.salliefeltonlifecoach.com

CHAPTER TWELVE

Develop a Disciplined Life

An interview with...

Dr. John Gray

DAVID WRIGHT (WRIGHT)

John, you've built a successful career as an expert giving relationship advice. I recently read a statement attributed to you: "A wise woman is careful not to pursue a man more than he is pursuing her." Will you explain why?

JOHN GRAY (GRAY)

When women make themselves too available to men, men get lazy. It's old-fashioned wisdom, but on a new level. We can understand it biochemically as well. Men bond with women when their testosterone levels go up. When there's a challenge, testosterone levels go up. But when things become easy, testosterone levels go down—so there needs to be a sense of the man initiating his own behaviors as to a woman doing it all.

The easiest way to make a man lose interest in you is to do everything for him. The most exciting thing to a man is when he feels that he is making a difference in a woman's life, as opposed to her doing everything for him.

WRIGHT

That makes sense. Perhaps definitions were different several years ago when I was single. Today, how does one determine if he or she is dating or in a "relationship"?

GRAY

Quite often women believe that when they are having sex with a man that they are having a monogamous relationship with him. They just assume that is his value system, and that's not always the case. I encourage women to assume that they're having a committed, monogamous relationship after a man has told them so.

The next question that comes up from women is, "Well, how do you bring up such a subject?" The best way to do it is to let him know at some point that you're not interested in having sex unless you're in an exclusive monogamous relationship. When he's ready to make that step she should tell him how she feels about it. That is certainly one approach.

WRIGHT

If someone is not sure that the person he or she is dating is "the one," how can that person get some help to sort through that uncertainty?

GRAY

Certainly feeling uncertain and doubting is a natural course of action in the dating process, and it's the first realization that's important. Sometimes people think, "If I don't know for sure, then maybe this is definitely not the right person for me."

One insight that is very important is that you could be with the right person for you, but still go through a period of feeling doubt and uncertainty. It's just a natural process, and while you are in that process it takes time before a part of you begins to sense that you're with the right person, or you begin to sense that you're with the wrong person. It just takes some time.

Couples who rush into making a commitment often make a mistake, and then feelings get hurt, so it's best to go slow when in doubt and not to assume that something's wrong.

WRIGHT

In the event of a cheating spouse or a lover, what should people do to learn to heal from infidelity in the relationship?

GRAY

It's an important concept to recognize that we all get our hearts broken, our partners make mistakes, and we experience disappointments. A part of growing in real love is the ability to forgive our partners for mistakes. People simply don't think sometimes and they make mistakes. By talking about it and sharing, people can understand what their mistakes are and make changes and grow from that. It's certainly a personal choice that some people make to simply exclude somebody who would ever cheat on them.

If someone has children I always encourage them to recognize that having an affair is a mistake, and people make mistakes—it's not a horrible, horrible mistake, it's just a mistake.

If someone's violent (that's more of a horrible, horrible mistake), even then it's forgivable if the person was to get help and recognize that he (or she) has a problem and overcome that problem.

The main question about being with someone is that after you have opened your heart and you've been hurt, if you take time to heal your heart, do you still want to be with him or her? That's the question. It's not for me or any other person to tell you whether you should be with that person; it's always an individual choice within the heart. The problem is that some people get caught up in this thinking that if someone makes a mistake then for sure I don't want to be with them. It's quite unrealistic to ever expect perfection in this world.

WRIGHT

In your writings you suggest using a relationship advisor or coach for those who need help. Will you explain the process?

GRAY

The process is simply talking with somebody who will ask you questions to help you to get in touch with your feelings. You can express your feelings without feeling that you're going to be judged or your feelings are going to hurt somebody or you're going to be held accountable and stand by those feelings. Often feelings need some room to flow and change as you grow in awareness. It's often not safe to show this with someone you're in a relationship with—the person might hold you to those feelings. So you go to a counselor to talk about those things.

Today it's becoming very popular to talk to coaches as well. One of the differences between a counselor and a coach is that a counselor is trained more academically in the process of analyzing what dysfunction you might have, and in providing a means to reflect on what's happening in your life related to things in your past. The counselor might even do more work on your childhood to rebuild self-esteem issues.

A coach is someone who is there to hold you accountable to do the things that you say you want to do by asking you questions. A coach can also become a sounding board who will ask you about what your feelings are, what happened, what you think should happen, what you think should not have happened, and what you think can happen. This type of exploration helps people find within themselves the wisdom to make better choices in their life. It also helps to motivate them to make better choices and follow up with action. So the coach tends to be more practically oriented.

A Mars/Venus coach adds to it an aspect of providing education as to the various insights of how men and women are different, how their emotional needs are different, and how they can motivate each other to be the best they can be in a relationship, rather than unknowingly pulling out the worst about the individuals in a relationship. I'm a big believer in education first, and then in coaching to motivate people. But often people don't even know what's going on, and some basic insights can help them make better choices and decisions. A coach can then assist them in staying motivated to achieve that end.

WRIGHT

I've heard the divorce rate is 50 percent. Is that true? And can a counselor or relationship coach actually help save a marriage?

GRAY

I've seen counselors ruin marriages, and I've seen counselors help save marriages. There are different forms of therapy. If you're in therapy and it doesn't feel right to you and you don't feel like you're making progress, you're probably in the wrong kind of therapy for you. There are some kinds of therapy where the opportunity is created for two people to sit and talk about how they feel with each other. This can result in arguments and fights in the counseling room just like the fights they have at home.

My Mars/Venus counselors are trained in ways to assist individuals in learning new ways of interacting, new ways of expressing their feelings, and new ways of avoiding arguments and fights. I think this is very important for a therapist to do. A Mars/Venus coach is going to focus more on assisting individuals in taking responsibility for how they're contributing to the problems in their relationship. This can simply be having someone to talk with to share what you're feeling. Sharing your feelings can sometimes bring about enormous insight into a situation, as well as helping you to feel better.

When you feel better you're able to respond in a more positive way. Our Mars/Venus coaches and counselors repeatedly receive stories and testimonials of couples who feel that their marriages were saved.

WRIGHT

I went on your Web site and I looked at some of the things that you're doing. I was really impressed. One thing that caught my eye was the Relationship Test. Does the Mars/Venus Relationship Test really work? What do you actually test?

GRAY

There are different areas of relationships which could be stronger or weaker. What a Relationship Test does is allows you to become more aware of what you're experiencing every day. Often people do not take the time to sit down and reflect on what's working here and what's not working. Our lives are often so busy that we're just going from the *next* thing to the *next* thing to the *next* thing, and we don't sit back and reflect on what's working and what's not working.

By doing the test and answering the questions, you're having to take that time and reflect upon what really is going on in your relationship. The irony in relationships is sometimes couples will be fighting in counseling or they'll be fighting at home, and they don't even know what they are fighting about. They don't even know how the argument started! Everything was fine, and suddenly one little thing happens and one or the other is flying off the handle and they just don't know what to do about it.

Often these flying off the handle experiences are like the water boiling and turning into steam. Long before it boiled, it simmered, and long before it simmered, the water was heating up. So there's a process that leads up to uncontrolled experiences in relationships. When you become more aware of what's not working in a relationship long before it's boiling, you have a chance to easily make adjustments in your behavior.

When taking a Relationship Test you're able to see many places where you have confusion or you don't understand what is going on. Talking to a relationship coach you can ask questions, particularly in the problem areas. You can talk about what's going on so that you can make sense of what's going on in your relationship.

Often when we don't know what's happening or don't know how to correctly interpret what's happening because it doesn't make sense to us, we then assume the worst rather than assume the best. And what our Mars/Venus coaches do is help to point out the *good* reasons why people do what they do, and strategies to help bring out the best in them.

WRIGHT

Every time I hear a talk show host ask a guest about the most important attribute a person needs to have when considering a relationship, the answer from males or females are always the same: "A good sense of humor." Is that really true?

GRAY

Well, that's what everybody says, but when difficulties arise in relationships the women then complain that the men are not serious. Or the man could complain that the woman isn't serious. Generally it's the number one thing on the list for women to say "a man's sense of humor," and when I hear that I want them to educate that woman to recognize that she's looking for the wrong thing. The last thing you need is for a man to entertain you. What you want is a man to provide security for you, to be attentive to you, and to understand you. In that place of safety, then you will naturally be expressive of your femininity, which is actually quite entertaining to men. It's the woman who brings joy to life, not the man. So when women are looking for men to bring joy to their life, women are often just feeling insecure as though they can't provide enough, and they are looking to a man to provide that role.

I have a wife and three daughters. When I travel with them it's amazing how entertaining they are! The nature of femininity is that women talk, they share, they look, they comment, they respond, they laugh a lot.

But what *is* good for a woman to look for in a man is not entertainment. She may think she's looking for that, but she'll find herself being disappointed again and again. What she should be looking for is a man's sense of humor in that he doesn't take things too seriously. That's extremely very attractive to women. Not taking himself too seriously means that he's not defensive about things and he doesn't claim to be perfect or expect or demand that she believes him to be perfect. That is a very healthy attitude and attribute in a man. If he can, in a sense, "lighten up," that constitutes a good sense of humor. That is what creates a sense of security for a woman.

If women want men to entertain them all the time, not only will they be disappointed, but it puts way too much pressure on men—they'll come on really strong and then women will lose interest because men are just not entertainers.

WRIGHT

Is it possible to be too cautious setting your criteria too high when choosing a life partner?

GRAY

I think the idea that you are getting at is very healthy to examine. I hesitate to say, "Lower your expectations and find your ideal partner." That sounds like you're not getting the best. What is going on today with both women and men is that they have very unrealistic expectations of what they require and what they want in a partner.

Life is often a gradual process of humbling them and helping them recognize what's realistic and what they are really looking for. We often look to the cover of a book rather than to the substance of the book, hence the old saying, "Don't judge a book by its cover." In our society we have become somewhat superficial in how we look for people. It takes a little maturing before we begin to realize who a person is is much more than how they look or how they react in certain situations or what they have or what they can do.

And yet those are all a part of the picture. I focus on helping couples change their expectations just in a sense of what a healthy relationship looks like. It doesn't mean that he's being romantic all the time, and it doesn't mean that she's happy all the time—two people really need to learn how to be happy on their own and then want to share that happiness with someone. That becomes the foundation of a relationship. When we are looking to someone to fill us up and make us happy, we will be disappointed later on. When we are somewhat happy and fulfilled in our own life, then we can find extra happiness through sharing our happiness with someone else. When that happens we are much less needy and our expectations tend to be much more realistic automatically.

WRIGHT

Almost everything you've said has hit me personally, especially the aspect of education. You see people who say, "This is my life-long partner" and they talk about all kinds of things, but it seems like you're talking about education.

GRAY

I feel that what's missing most in the world today when it comes to relationships is insight and education into understanding how to create healthy relationships. And why we need this education now more so than a hundred years ago, is that people didn't take courses even fifty years ago in improving their relationships. That's because there were hundreds of years of tradition where women had certain roles and men had certain roles. Men interacted in certain ways and women interacted in certain ways. As long as everybody acted according to those established patterns, everyone got along quite well.

Then the world changed. Now the world is different and yet no one has defined new roles and how men and women are supposed to interact and what works best for them. To a certain extent there is no "best"—it's a world of tremendous freedom and choice and we have to define those roles ourselves. But in defining those roles there's a certain amount of freedom to create those roles, and there's also a certain lack of freedom.

I might wish to walk through a wall, but I just can't—certain realities don't change. So in this world where we are "making up" relationships in a new way, there are certain realities that have not changed. There are certain ways that men interact and there are certain ways that women interact. There are certain needs that women have and certain needs that men have. The needs men and women have are different. By understanding those differences we can then realistically work with those differences to support each other better at this time of enormous change and enormous stress in our lives due to that change.

And what is interesting is that men and women react differently to stress, so most of the differences that cause frustration between men and women are simply differences that we don't understand, and those differences that we don't instinctively relate to are particularly how men and women react to stress.

For example, men will often become quiet or distant under stress, whereas women will want to open up and share and talk under stress. And then, taking another step that stresses even more, women will then *not* want to talk because they'll feel that they've tried to talk and no one listened so they begin to close up, and then they have no way to effectively cope with stress.

On the other hand, you've got men who tend to naturally pull away and mull things over to feel better under stress. If they are really under a huge amount of stress, these men don't even take the time to pull away. They go into a more talkative mode—they just want to complain and point out how they are victims in life. This becomes very distressing to women, and they go further and further away. That's what I would call "role reversal," which is another problem occurring today.

There are a lot of combinations in men and women and we just don't understand how to make sense of it, but by having a basic understanding of how men and women are different and how they cope with stress differently, we can then be better equipped to support our partners when they are under a lot of stress.

For example, if my wife doesn't want to talk about something, I can be helpful to her and be cooperative, which will lower her stress level. She will then begin to open up and talk, which will lower her stress level even more—as long as I make it safe for her to talk.

If a man is stressed and is complaining a lot and talking a lot, then what a woman can do is instead of trying to be a good listener, she can simply ask him to talk with his friends and give her some room to do what she wants to do. She should not encourage him to talk about all the things that are going wrong in his life. As she leaves him alone he will then be able to cope with stress better. He will then "come out of his cave" so to speak and be much friendlier to her. Women have to recognize that when men are in a bad mood or when they're stressed out, it's not up to her to do anything for him. Men have to come out of this primarily on their own; otherwise they tend to become weak.

So these are primary differences that a woman wouldn't think of. Another example is if a woman's feeling stressed out and he comes to her and asks her questions to help open her up and give her support, it will actually empower her. And doing so empowers the man. But when a woman is too much like a mother to a man, it will weaken him and she will resent it later as well, that's a no-win situation.

WRIGHT

I have known you for several years and I have always been impressed by your ability to stay on the leading edge of the subjects you are passionate about. Have you found any new information about relationship-building in the past few of years that might help people make fewer mistakes in the search for love and companionship?

GRAY

I think that in a sense I was touching on that a few minutes ago when I mentioned the subject of stress. Stress has become so high that not only do men and women have strong stress reactions, they actually go further into a role reversal where women are so stressed that they feel they have to do everything themselves and they become very much like a man. Men become so stressed that they begin to complain about their lives and feel like they're not responsible for their lives anymore. This is the wrong direction, and yet it's a natural stress reaction.

Today we are experiencing unprecedented amounts of stress with longer commuting hours and higher costs of living, balancing work and home life, increased information, and cell phones, talking, and being connected to work all the time. All this is putting a huge new burden on our lives and on our relationships.

What I have done is help to point this out, which can help couples enormously. Couples can recognize that there are ways to lower stress. If we are going to have more dramatic stress, there are more dramatic ways that couples can lower the stress levels for each other. Those ways happen to be women learning to ask for help—that's a real big issue—and men being more responsive to give help. That's not to say they have to do it every time she asks as if he's supposed to "jump to it." There are times when you are supposed to take your rest, so there needs to be understanding of that.

Women often resent having to ask for help, and that is something that has to change. She has to recognize that when you grow up in this world you have to learn how to ask for things, particularly in the business world. Likewise in relationships, if a woman wants her partner to change his natural mode of behavior she needs to *ask*. She shouldn't expect him to be like a woman who would just tend to think about everything that needs to be done until overwhelmed doing it—men typically don't fall into that role. So she needs to ask him, and when people ask others to do something, when they do it they need to let them know it's appreciated.

This is a new skill for a woman. While women sometimes resist this, once they practice it they realize, "Wow, this isn't that hard, and it works!" So that's one way to lower stress in life—if women are not feeling supported to *ask* for it in a way that will work rather than the way that they do ask, which often doesn't work. Practice "realistic expectations." Instead of complaining that "I can't walk through this wall" and "Why doesn't the wall open up for me?" you've got to find the door and learn how to open it!

The second important area to lower stress is in the realm of communication. Women want more sharing and more communication and men aren't providing that. There's a way that men can provide it—if women cooperate. As I said before, women should ask for what they want. Maybe a woman could say something like, "I'd like for you to listen to what is going on in my life." Let him know that he doesn't have to say anything. In fact, I encourage that in the beginning—he should say nothing, and let her talk for five or ten minutes. She then thanks him for listening, and then walks away. While this seems very unnatural, it is a super stress reducer once people start to experience it. It's quite amazing.

I didn't invent this—this is what has been going on for years in the therapy office. Women come in and they talk about what's going on in their lives and they feel better. The therapist doesn't say much at all. And the better the therapist, the less the therapist says and the more questions the therapist asks.

So the secret here is learning how to talk about what is bothering you without expecting a solution or without expecting your partner to "fix" you or fix the situation in some way. So she can set up that conversation and she will feel better; he'll feel better too because he helped her. And men like helping their wives.

The third area is romance. Again, in this area couples stopped having romance, and romance is actually one of the most strong and powerful stress reducers. It's just that when we're under stress the last thing we think about is romance, both for her and for him. Yet the difference is women will often think about how much they miss it. They're not necessarily feeling romantic, but they often complain that "he's not romantic," implying that she wants him to be romantic so she can feel good again. I understand that and I respect that. And I have a solution for that, but it's not waiting for him—you have to ask! Now, what woman would ever think to ask for romance? Well *you* can. It's a very simple thing.

To solve this problem women have to learn how to ask, and men have to learn how to respond. Women then have to learn how to appreciate that, and the solutions do occur. Women can't expect a man to be a mind-reader. He doesn't know what's going on inside her head and in her heart. Asking for romance is something so foreign that women need a few examples of it and then they can get the hang of it.

For example, she shouldn't say, "You're not romantic, we don't experience romance anymore, we never go out anymore, we're not having fun anymore." Those are just negative complaints. Instead she needs to focus more on what's positive. For example, "Hey, this particular band is playing in town this weekend. Would you get tickets for the concert?" The woman asks the man—that's it. It's a very simple thing. The woman could say, "Oh, we haven't gone out this week, would you get tickets for this or that?" or simply, "Would you pick a movie and we'll go see the movies?" or "Would you make reservations and let's go out to eat?" The man could say, "Where would you like to go?" The woman could say, "Whatever you want to pick."

Women can start defining romance as letting him decide where to go, her asking for it, him deciding, and her having a good time just being with him! And gradually that moves into more discretion about what you're going to do and so forth. This process will begin to restore the woman's confidence in the man. All the woman needs to do is to just ask and let him know that whatever he does will be fine.

Just as it was in the beginning when he was so romantic, men often become unromantic because they try, but after a while women start picking out what he did wrong. And men will think, "Well she's so picky I'll just let her decide." And that's the end of romance because part of what reduces stress for women is that she does not have to decide. And when a woman comes back to the realization that having the man make some decisions and she doesn't have to decide will actually lower her stress enormously. It also lowers a man's stress enormously when he knows that whatever he decides she's going to like, as opposed to feeling that he's going to put his best out there and she's going to step all over it by pointing out what he did wrong. She doesn't mean to do that, but that's the net effect.

So these are extra additions, extra awareness's, and insights that can help couples to cope with the extra stress they're experiencing in their lives today.

WRIGHT

If you had to "bottom line" the reasons for the success of your Mars and Venus books, products, ideas, and counseling help, what would the main reason be?

GRAY

I think that because the world has changed, people are eager and hungry to have a new way of understanding the world in a positive light. When we don't understand what is going on around us, we just assume something's wrong. By learning the new insights regarding how men and women are different, and how we look at the world differently in a *positive* way, they are released from having to blame their partners or blame themselves. They are motivated to find creative solutions that make their relationships better. So in one aspect, what I do is give people permission to make mistakes, and give them insight to solve the problems.

WRIGHT

An interesting conversation! I always learn so much when I talk with you. It's just incredible. I really do appreciate this time that you've spent with me today, and I really think the readers are going to get a lot out of it.

GRAY

Well, thank you so much. It's a pleasure.

ABOUT THE AUTHOR

Dr. John Gray is the author of fifteen books, including *Men Are from Mars, Women Are from Venus* (Harper Collins 1992), a number one best-selling relationship book. Over thirty million Mars and Venus books have been sold in over forty languages throughout the world.

Dr. John Gray, a certified family therapist, is the premier Better Life relationship coach on AOL. In 2001, he received the Smart Marriages Impact Award. John Gray received his degree in 1982 from Columbia Pacific University. He has authored fourteen other best-selling books. His book, *The Mars & Venus Diet & Exercise Solution* (St. Martin's Press 2003), reveals why diet, exercise, and communication skills combine to effect the production of healthy brain chemicals and how the need for those chemicals differ between men and women.

An internationally recognized expert in the fields of communication and relationships, Dr. Gray's unique focus is assisting men and women in understanding, respecting, and appreciating their differences. For decades, he has conducted public and private seminars for thousands of participants. In his highly acclaimed books, audiotapes, and videotapes, as well as in his seminars, Dr. Gray entertains and inspires audiences with his practical insights and easy to use communication techniques that can be immediately applied to enrich relationships and quality of life.

Dr. Gray lives with his wife and three children in Northern California.

John Gray
www.askmarsvenus.com

CHAPTER THIRTEEN
Your Personal "GPS"

An interview with...

Dr. Michael O'Connor

DAVID WRIGHT (WRIGHT)

We are most pleased that Dr. Michael O'Connor is here to share his profound insights about how we can optimize our personal success in ways that work best for each of us. As a recognized *thought leader* and author of books published in more than twenty languages, his timeless insights and practical applications continue to benefit people worldwide. Dr. O'Connor is known as a practical problem-solving visionary who has successfully applied this "know-how" daily throughout his career as a business owner, business advisor, executive, coach, professor, and speaker dedicated to helping people win in life.

Dr. O'Connor, welcome. The variety of your contributions is most fascinating with their breadth, depth, and continuing transformation through today's computer-enabled technologies. Let's begin our conversation by explaining for the readers what the "Personal GPS" that you created is and how it fits with the concept of a GPS for success, which is the focus of this book.

DR. MICHAEL O'CONNOR (O'CONNOR)

The commonality is that both are "life guides" designed for helping us orient, focus, and achieve our desired destination. Specifically, in terms of the Personal GPS, this involves gaining clarity about 1) where we have been, 2) where we are currently in our life, 3) where we want to go, and then 4) how to successfully accomplish this.

It is a comprehensive, integrated system for understanding the "total person," which took me more than thirty years of formal and applied research with people, teams, and organizations to fully develop. It enables us to have a strong, useable understanding of both ourselves and others that is vital for both our personal success and satisfaction. This is more crucial now than ever, due to the increasing stresses, demands, pace, and disruptions in our personal and work lives. In this stressful time we are at continuing risk both for our personal well-being and success as well as that of our groups/teams and organizations.

Earlier in my career I used these concepts in my practice and with pencil-and-paper assessment tools. By computerizing both the assessments and the interpreted results, this made it easier, quicker, and more effective for clients and me. Based on this experience, the next phase was to share it with other professionals and their organizations for clients and finally, for individual consumers. So these behavioral concepts are now easily, quickly, and successfully replicated and used by people for a variety of applications through a suite of online assessment and development tools.

For instance, these tools identify a person's "fit" with current and future roles. Here is an example. An international recreational products company asked me to assess the performance of their sales force as part of a strategic shift required for their future business success. We identified the high performance profile for various key positions and then assessed both current and prospective jobholders for these positions. The result was a dramatic increase in both the quality of selected candidates and sales performance. In fact, one of their sales managers, who had been discounted for a key sales executive opportunity, was discovered to be a potential super-star through this process. As a result, he was reconsidered and ultimately given that leadership opportunity. Since that time he has developed a corporate-wide reputation as not only a stellar sales executive, but a brilliant coach whose use of the GPS concepts, tools, and related performance management practices have become a model that other managers and divisions have since adopted.

WRIGHT

So, in summary what are the key benefits an individual or organization can gain from using this Personal GPS that you say is vital for our success?

O'CONNOR

For individuals, it helps make our life work for us on our own terms so that we are not only more successful but also more fulfilled. For organizations, it's a practical tool for further unleashing and focusing both the energy and talents that generate much greater productivity and satisfaction. In addition, a real bonus for organizations is that it provides a much faster, more cost effective process along with significantly higher success rates than common interviewing practices, non-integrated assessments, or paper-and-pencil instruments.

For instance, in the area of selection, a variety of research studies has shown success rates of just 8 percent to 25 percent and an enormous cost to organizations for lost time in rehiring along with lost revenue gains from hiring lower performers. When used properly as part of a sound selection process, the GPS has had at least a 75 percent success rate.

WRIGHT

What are the most common, high impact practical applications for the Personal GPS know-how and tools?

O'CONNOR

It can be used to increase the likelihood of our success and satisfaction in both our work life and non-work, personal life.

For instance, at work it is typically used for a variety of communication applications such as positively influencing people (whether co-workers, your boss, or customers), increasing personal effectiveness, improving teamwork, coaching and managing performers, high performance job analysis, employee and management selection, performance management and development, career pathing, and succession planning.

Here is one of the many testimonials from people who attended our "Hiring & Developing Winners" program. This one is from the General Manager of an organization:

> "When I attended your *Hiring Winners Workshop* I did not know what to expect. I cannot put a price on the knowledge and tools I left with. We had been struggling to get good techs, service writers, and good employees overall. We had recently built a costly new facility with eight service bays and could not seem to find good techs to fill it. Of the ones we did hire, a large percentage did not work out. Your workshop taught me how to profile different positions and what transferable capabilities and motivations in performers that we should be looking for. I also learned how to better attract qualified people and, most importantly, how

to interview properly by focusing on what really counts to find out if this is really the right person *before* we hire them!

Since attending the workshop I have hired a service manager, three service writers, two lot porters, and seven more techs. It has been two years and they have all worked out fantastically! Our service manager truly manages the entire department, the service writers are the best I have ever had, and our techs are achieving excellent collectable efficiencies and quality of work.

Our [financial] numbers have almost doubled from our previous peak and my own involvement in the department's day-to-day operations has gone from excessive to non-existent. Even in the height of the busy season, our service department is able to say yes to servicing every customer's equipment, no matter where they bought it. Most of the new employees came from other industries but already had superior transferable capabilities, the motivations, and adaptability that allowed them to migrate to our industry with ease.

Now our people really are our most valuable asset! Thank you so much for helping us discover how to make this happen."

The Personal GPS concept and tools are equally, if not more, essential and valuable in our personal, non-work lives. People use it for many similar applications in these settings, situations, and relationships. These include our communication practices, increasing compatibility and reducing conflict with others, improving their personal effectiveness with people and at managing tasks, and strengthening their decision-making and personal life management.

WRIGHT

What is unique about the Personal GPS system that makes it so much more powerful than other resources for personal as well as interpersonal effectiveness and satisfaction?

O'CONNOR

A while ago, a widely-acclaimed meta-analysis that identified the performance dimensions among people was referred to as the "Big 5." However, a review of it by my co-author and research colleague, Dr. Drea Zigarmi, and me indicated that it actually included only three of what we refer to as the "Big 6," which comprise our Personal GPS with a more comprehensive view of people.

This is extremely important since most other models, as well as personal assessment users, over-simplify, over-generalize, and therefore too often misdiagnose the driving factors that explain our own and others' personal actions.

By contrast, the GPS identifies the specific types of *motivations* that explain what people will and won't do *as well as* the different types of *capabilities* that identify what people can and can't do! And, people can both readily learn this model and practically apply it in their daily lives to understand why they and others do what they do as well as how to apply and develop the capabilities needed for success in working with the variety of people we have to deal with in both our work and personal lives!

The 'Big 6' Job Performance Factors

CAPABILITIES	MOTIVATION
1. Job-Specific Capabilities	4. Personal Work Style
2. Transferable Capabilities	5. Work Values (Beliefs)
3. Adaptability	6. Work Interests

Because it integrates both a total set of *motivations* and *capabilities* factors, it differs from other tools and approaches in its ability to diagnose the root causes of our behavior, including performance (or non-performance) and role fits.

For example, about three years ago, my colleague, David Spader, was working with a young woman who had joined their family business. She and her father were experiencing much more unresolved conflict than was either necessary or in their own and the business's best interests. The father called David in to see if he could help them work together.

We conducted a 360 degree assessment of both the father and the daughter. The daughter's results showed a very high role fit for all three types of required capabilities for her position (Job Specific, Transferable, and Adaptability). She was also a high fit by her personal work style drives and tendencies. However, when we looked at her personal values, there was only a moderate fit for her current role, and a lower fit for managerial type work.

Yet, the true root issue wasn't her personal values, but, instead, her personal interests. Her interests revealed a very low fit with the type of work she was doing and would be required to do in the future if she took over management of this family business.

After exploring this with her, for the first time she realized that she didn't like the type of work this required of her. The revealing moment came when, with tears streaming down her face she said, "I think the only reason I wanted to run the family business was because ever since I can remember Grandpa always said that I would take over the family business. I don't want to disappoint Grandpa." Fortunately, when her father discovered this, he responded wisely by saying, "You know Grandpa would only want you to be happy and fulfilled in life."

We then developed an action plan for her to go back to school in an area for which she had very strong personal interests.

Three years later, David received an e-mail message one morning that said, "I have wanted to reconnect with you and let you know I really appreciate the tools you have given me in realizing how to improve my life through goal-setting and challenging my natural tendencies. Thank you very much, David. Sorry it took me so long to get back to you. I want you to know you have made a huge impact on my life."

WRIGHT

Describe the different *motivations* that identify "why we do what we do" based on your decades of formal and applied research, consulting, and coaching with people. Include important differences these make for success in our life.

O'CONNOR

Each of us is motivated at any one point in time or situation by our needs, values, or interests. However, at any point in time, only one of these will be the primary driving source causing us to do what we do in that situation. That said, let's look at each of these three motivators that helps us demystify why people do what they do. Then we will look at an example of all three in action in another real-life situation.

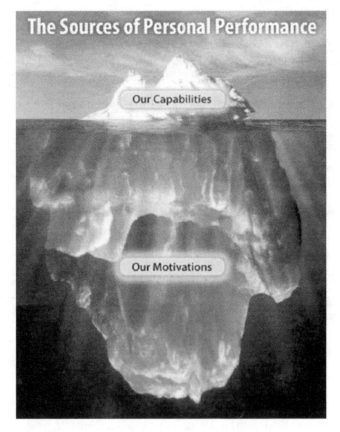

Our *needs* are motivated patterns describing what we naturally do in a situation. A variety of observers and researchers of human behavior, across cultures from ancient times to the present, have identified four primary natural habit patterns among people. These patterns differ in terms of being either more *direct/extroverted* acting or *indirect/introverted* acting. They involve the motivation to either *control* situations (including those where people are involved) or *relate* in situations.

People have a natural core needs-based temperament early in life. Our research has shown that 80 percent of adults have developed at least one secondary pattern that describes them, most commonly because of their work role requirements. In our Personal GPS system, we refer to these four primary patterns or personal styles as:

1. Dominant Director (Direct and Controlling habits, tendencies)
2. Interacting Socializers (Direct and Relating habits, tendencies)
3. Steady Relaters (Indirect and Relating habits, tendencies)
4. Cautious Thinkers (Indirect and Controlling habits, tendencies)

Among the common uses of this model is its most frequent application relative to interpersonal communications and compatibility. For instance, people with similar patterns tend to attract and be comfortable with each other socially, while likes tend to compete or conflict. However, in the work setting, those with different tendencies are more likely to complement the required work practices of others with different tendencies. This dimension of motivation is often then used to improve communications with others, teamwork, and personal effectiveness in situations. An example is for both better task and people performance. The stories are too numerous to mention. If interested, I refer you to another book I have co-authored on this subject, *People Smart,* which is listed in the bibliography at the end of this chapter.

By contrast, our *values* describe what either we or others believe we should do in a situation. It is important to note that any of the four types of Personal Styles (DISC) can be found with any of these four values patterns. Once again, cross-cultural research throughout history has verified four different types of patterns. Each has its own unique type of positive, goal-driven aspiration and, when negatively-motivated its own more fear-driven, counter-productive views and actions.

While this dimension was not very popular when I did my own formal academic research in this field in the 1970s era, it has recently become popularized by marketers and others in speaking of differing generational values (for instance, Generations X, Y, Z) by various individuals, including a brilliant and respected co-author of mine for this dimension of behavior, Dr. Morris Massey.

Regardless of names, the patterns remain the same across the ages, recurring in identifiable cyclical patterns, and each with its own motivators, strengths, and development opportunities. In our Personal GPS system, we refer to them as:

- Individualists (Challenging point of view)
- Seekers (Searching, In-Between point of view)
- Conventionalists (Traditional point of view)
- Integrators (Synthesizing point of view)

Our *interests* are the third type of motivation that explains why we do what we do. These are the personal likes and dislikes that describe what we are both passionate about (our interests) and strongly seek to avoid (our disinterests). An example was noted previously regarding the young lady whose disinterests caused her to bypass the opportunity to take over their family business.

There are two basic types of interests among people: *people* or *things*—each with other sub-sets of these, resulting in a field of twelve different types of personal interests. Once again, it is worth noting that we have found from our work with people that nearly two out of three people have different patterns for their work versus non-work life interests! We have also discovered that beneath our interests are specific types of underlying needs or values that cause us to "dislike" or "like" these.

This information is vital for understanding members of any group, whether a work group, management team, or family (including prospective members). For example, I have seen numerous examples of naturally-occurring conflicts between people in work and personal life situations based on conflicting *needs*-based personal style tendencies.

We have time and again provided coaching to help people readily resolve such situations by increasing each other's understanding, appreciation, and more effective practices at interacting with each other. I have also seen the same, including when people have different personal *interests*, for instance, in assessing role and tasks fit and how to best manage these.

The toughest incompatibilities are when people have different personal values. This is usually manifested when one person has a strong point of view about what he or she thinks is best, right, or important and another party has an equally strong differing view or is not responsive to the first person's strong motivating beliefs.

An example I remember to this day involved two business partners. Both had strong natural controlling tendencies (Dominant Director with different secondary style tendencies). However, while this contributed to tensions, this was an area I was able to help them minimize. Similarly, both had higher status interests in their work life. However, over time this was further strained by one partner's strong "economic (financial) interest" that too frequently cost him due to the other partner's "entrepreneurial" interest.

This partnership did not last, as they parted ways after several years. The root cause for their separation was failure to reconcile their personal values differences. More specifically, the more "Traditional" partner finally decided he'd "had enough" when his "Seeker" partner sought to "unilaterally change his mind" (and their written, legal partnership agreement) to pursue another in his series of unending entrepreneurial and status interests. The deal-breaker was his doing so without consideration of their pre-existing agreement or subsequent mutual agreement to change it (a defensive flight pattern).

WRIGHT

When people talk about different personal styles or values, many seem to think some are better or more preferable than others. What does the research and your work show about this?

O'CONNOR

In a given situation, one style or values perspective is likely to be more appropriate than another based upon what that situation requires for successful results. However, across the range of different types of situations there is *no* single, best pattern of either personal styles or values. Nonetheless, it is common for people to have a tendency to think their own personal style or values point of view is what's best. Therefore, people tend to judge least favorably those patterns that differ most from their own.

As a general guiding principle, a person who is more positively goal- and growth-motivated is likely to produce better results for both themselves and others than a person who is negatively motivated. As such, negative attitudes and actions are characterized by defensive types of "fight or flight" behaviors.

WRIGHT

How does *self-esteem* relate to this variety of motivational and behavior patterns and how significant is it for our success and satisfaction?

O'CONNOR

Individuals with higher *self-esteem* are, by definition, those individuals I've been describing as more positively-motivated individuals who tend to be more growth-focused in their attitudes and actions, while negatively driven people are resistant to change and characterized by fight or flight responses.

No one has total or perfect high esteem. In other words, he or she is likely to vary by both individual as well as personal situations. When tired, distressed, overwhelmed, less self-confident, or conflicted, any of us are likely to demonstrate lower esteem characteristics. So, our esteem level can vary.

It's important to distinguish between which of the two different dimensions of esteem is involved when this occurs. The first is our sense of one another's worth, which is most closely related to whether we have had a personal life history of having our needs met. The second is our sense of respect for self and others, which is most closely related to whether we value ourself and others.

So, we have indeed found that individuals with higher *esteeming* attitudes and behaviors (toward both self and others) are much more likely to view and respond to experiences in a more positive, proactive approach. By contrast, those characterized by lower self-esteem overall, or in a given situation, are more likely to view and respond to such in a more negative, reactive type of either flight or fight defensive behavior pattern.

It is important to understand this for a number of practical reasons. We can develop higher self-esteem in our lives (and contribute to the same for others). The difference is that negative, more anxiety/fear-based actions involve coping practices among people. By contrast, more positive, goal-focused attitudes and actions involve a growth state. A second key principle, based on this reality, is that none of the three motivational patterns (needs, values, or interests) are inherently "better" than the others within or between these!

The impact of our self-esteem in shaping our perceptions and responses to situations and circumstances in our lives is pervasive as well as deep. For instance, two people who differ in their self-esteem are likely to see the same situation as either a problem to protect, defend their self from (lower esteem response), or an opportunity for breakthrough (higher esteem response). I've seen many executives for whom their self-confidence, whether unrealistically higher or lower, has had a significant impact on their personal success and life.

It also shows in such areas as our personal career choices. For example, I know of a President and majority owner of a business who discovered that his work motivations (work style, interests) matched up better as an "individual contributor" versus "managerial role." As a result, this person retained his owner role but turned over his management role to others who were a better fit, as this owner pursued his individual contributor specialized role. As a result, both productivity and morale increased and was sustained as his talents were optimized and problems were significantly reduced.

WRIGHT

Regarding the *capabilities* dimension of the Personal GPS, what are the different types and how do these differ?

O'CONNOR

For many people, the term "capabilities" is a buzz word. However, in the Personal GPS system, it refers to a person's capacity to be successful in a specific situation based on the knowledge, skills, and/or experience he or she has developed and demonstrated. Three types of capabilities are assessed for strength and development where called for. They are:

- Job-specific knowledge, skills, experience
- Transferable knowledge, skills, experience
- Adaptability

Job-specific "know-how" represents the types of capabilities that are most commonly focused on by employers in their effort to determine whether candidates are qualified for a job. However, research has shown that while it is a threshold requirement for especially more complex jobs, it is not sufficient for predicting performance. In other words, you wouldn't be likely to hire anyone as a computer repair technician without a level of knowledge and skills in this area. However, by itself this will not allow you to determine whether candidates will be minimally acceptable, average, or higher performers in this job. Instead, higher capabilities performance for most jobs is better predicted by transferable capabilities.

Transferable capabilities include a variety of task-focused competencies in areas such as task management, decision-making, and processes management. It also consists of more people-based capabilities like influencing, self-management, and people management. This includes mixed capabilities such as communications, problem-solving, and leadership.

The third type of capabilities are the ones most critical for roles and situations that involve change, ambiguity, adversity, complexity, and conflict. These include a fast increasing number of jobs such as managerial and leadership. We refer to this third type of capabilities as *Adaptability*. It consists of two dimensions. One is *Flexibility*, a series of attitudes that describe our willingness to change—being approachable and open to other ideas, possibilities. The second dimension is *Versatility*, a set of aptitudes that describe our ability to effectively deal with change and difficulties. Among these capabilities are agility, sound risk-taking, and ability to respond appropriately to situations.

One of the most interesting job analyses that I recall involved field repair technicians for heavy construction equipment. Historically, such individuals had been hired for their job-specific technical know-how. However, the performance among them varied significantly despite similar levels of technical knowledge. Upon further review, it was discovered that among the other key predictors of higher performance were their problem-solving and achievement capabilities—both of which are different from, and independent of, a person's technical knowledge. Selecting and developing people with this profile for higher performance became a significant asset for that business for this and other jobs where they applied this more comprehensive assessment of job capabilities.

WRIGHT

Of these three types of *capabilities* in our current and emerging world, is there one that is more important for people to develop, and if so, why?

O'CONNOR

Adaptability—both flexibility (our willingness to change) and versatility (our ability to change)—is the most important. This is due to the increasing, unpredictable, and unfavorable types, pace, and variety of change in today's world, including situations so many people have not yet faced and in which they are therefore less likely to succeed.

Adaptability Model

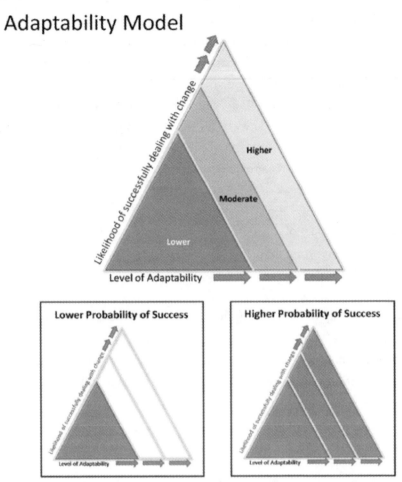

We recently saw this in a group of businesses in an industry experiencing a lot of consolidation. Even though the leaders in these businesses were quite strong in their Job Specific and Transferable Capabilities, they differed significantly with respect to their Adaptability. This one factor greatly differentiated the group in terms of the profitability of their organization's performance. The highest performing organizations were directed by leaders who were much more adaptable than the comparison companies, and their bottom line performance reflected this. We've seen Adaptability have a dramatic impact among organizations that have either increased in size or had a major shift in either their product/services or customer/marketplace base.

Among individuals we have found a very similar pattern. For example, time and again I've seen individuals who began with more Job-Specific Capability and even greater transferable strengths be passed by as they are outperformed by "High Adaptors" who are continually learning, growing, and, as a result, achieving better and better results at performing tasks and with people practices. One more increasing pattern we have noted among individuals involves those who were successful in the past who are now either struggling or failing as the requirements for success continue to change and become more demanding.

When working with professionals in groups/teams we often ask questions about their Adaptability such as, "How many of you like change?" Almost no hands go up. Or, "Do you think the world is changing faster or slower?" "Are customers getting more or less demanding?" "Are employees getting easier or more challenging to work with?" "Is your marketplace getting more or less complex?" "Is it getting easier or more difficult to predict the changes that are likely to occur?" In each case, their responses indicate that Adaptability is becoming a universal requirement for sustained individual and organizational success in our present and future world.

WRIGHT

So what's the "bottom line" for our own and others' personal success in life—to focus first on *capabilities* or on *motivations?*

O'CONNOR

Both my experience and research overwhelmingly indicate that the answer is *motivations.* One key reason is because our motivations shape and, in this respect, either expand or limit the degree and types of *capabilities* we both develop and put into successful action.

I've seen this repeatedly with different people. Those who are positively motivated focus on growing, getting better, and end up shaping a future that typically differs from their personal past success level and reflects substantial gains.

However, I also want to be clear about this. Specifically, for sustained personal success *both* are required—being motivated and not capable will not yield sustained success. Being capable but not positively motivated is a formula for personal self-destruction as shown by decades of research on "career derailment" factors among managers and executives, which is overwhelmingly due to "relationship" issues, not their task capabilities.

WRIGHT

Overwhelmingly, most assessments used with people are self-assessments. So, why do you put so much emphasis on both self and observers' assessments of an individual's Personal GPS?

O'CONNOR

Both are important, but the research and our decades of experience with self-assessments convincingly show that all types tend to reflect our "perception" but are not accurate representations of the reality of the behavior dimension assessed.

For example, a *Business Week* study showed that 90 percent of executives and senior managers view themselves as being in the top 10 percent of all such performers—an obvious mathematical impossibility of course.

We have seen this same pattern with our GPS assessments. Specifically, among higher managerial levels, individuals tend to have a much more favorable self-view than do others they select as knowing them well in that same setting. Most are both surprised—and displeased—when they see how others view them. The real winners accept this feedback, seek to understand it more clearly and deeply, and take action to strengthen their performance for either the *motivation* or *capability* dimension involved. By contrast, those who do not make any significant gains from this process tend to deny, rationalize, or otherwise pay lip service to such assessments rather than grow from this opportunity.

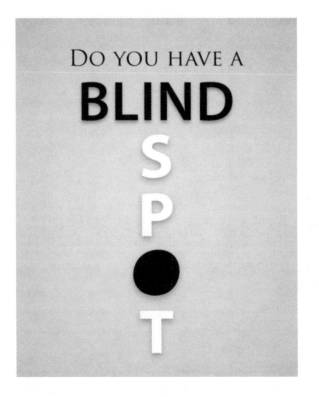

Our own GPS assessment database of several thousands of professionals over two decades indicate that at least 80 percent of people view themselves differently than those they select as knowing that dimension of their behavior in that setting.

Self-assessments are still important to identify people's "intentions" as well as how they think they are acting. However, this "blind spot" or not so "hidden agenda" self-view among 80 percent indicate that without assessments by others we are likely to be deluded about how we are actually viewed with respect to both our *motivations* and *capabilities* as well as how we are impacting others in our work and non-work lives.

The *Gap Analysis* between these differing views becomes the basis for practical GPS-based action plans to focus on for realigning those attitudes and/or practices that are most important for personal success and growth.

WRIGHT

As a recognized thought leader and best-selling author of books on leadership as well as organizational culture, is there a connection between an individual's Personal GPS and these two areas?

O'CONNOR

Yes. With respect to *leadership*, sustained success requires a sound, strong understanding of our strengths and key development opportunities. In fact, when one popular "research" study was published in a best-selling book, it advised leaders to focus only on their strengths and capitalize on these, not to be concerned with their undeveloped dimensions. So, I asked leaders who had successfully moved up the corporate ladder how they did so. They consistently reported that the way they were able to progress in their careers was by *both* capitalizing on their strengths *and* developing those other key strengths required for success in their position, then continuing to do so over time, whether in the same or different positions. They credited the Personal GPS and its predecessor tools as valuable resources for achieving their aspirations.

Recently, an organization had to dismiss a GM for inappropriate behavior. They had just become aware of how to use the GPS tools in the Hiring Winners process and used these tools to assess the successor candidates. After doing so, they settled on an internal candidate. While he wasn't a perfect fit, he demonstrated a very different set of motivations than his departed predecessor.

One year later, the organization reported a 181 percent improvement in the management team's alignment with the organization's values. The GM was the only change on the management team. Since this was done in conjunction with a company values-based *culture* initiative, not all of this dramatic improvement can be attributed to the GM. However, we know that the greatest single driver of organizational culture is an organization's people, especially its leadership team that sets a work culture's tone. Obviously, the new GM was very aligned with its core work values and both communicated and demonstrated the aligned performance expected for which other employees quickly, and quite uniformly followed suit.

In the area of culture, those organizations that are not just built to last but actually do are ones that are led, managed, and executed by individuals and teams that shared three common characteristics: 1) being proactive, positively motivated, forward-moving, growth-oriented, 2) being increasingly more capable, and 3) demonstrating effective commitment to a common set of business values that serve the mutual self-interests of their key stakeholder groups, including their own. My research and work in this area is found in the book I co-authored titled *Managing by Values* listed in the bibliography here.

Authored Resources

O'Connor, Michael with Tony Alessandra. *People Smart* (2009), Life Associates LLC.

O'Connor, Michael with Tony Alessandra, *The Platinum Rule* (1996), Warner Business Books.

O'Connor, Michael with Drea Zigarmi et al. *The Leader Within* (Sept. 2004), Prentice Hall.

O'Connor, Michael with Ken Blanchard. *Managing By Values,* 2nd Edition (Oct. 2003), Berrett-Koehler Publishers.

O'Connor, Michael with Sandra Merwin. *The Mysteries of Motivation* (1988), Life Associates LLC.

O'Connor, Michael with Deepak Chopra, Jack Canfield, Denis Waitley. *Stepping Stones to Success* (2010), Insight Publishing.

O'Connor, Michael. *The Global Profiles System* (On-line assessment and development tools). www.lifeassociatesinc.com.

O'Connor, Michael. Varied Archived Webinars On Motivation, Capabilities, and Managing Performance. www.lifeassociatesinc.com.

About the Author

Dr. Michael O'Connor is the Founder and Executive Vice President of Life Associates and The Center For Managing By Values. His more than thirty years of research and applied work has been translated into bestselling books listed among his credits. Michael is also the creator of the *GPS (Global Profiles System)*, which includes self, observer(s), and job analyses reports for both personal motivational and capabilities dimensions of performance. He holds a BS degree in the social sciences, an MA in the behavioral sciences/psychology, and a PhD in management. You can contact him through his Web site and access resources he has developed, including free webinars, at www.lifeassociatesinc.com.

Dr. Michael O'Connor
Founder
Life Associates
North Collier Corporate Center I
1004 Collier Center Way, Suite 106
Naples, FL 34110
Toll Free (877) 628-0028; (239) 947-1111
Fax (239) 254-1644
drmichaeloconnor@lifeassociatesinc.com
www.lifeassociatesinc.com

CHAPTER FOURTEEN
Professional Presence in a Casual World

An interview with...
Suzanne Updegraff

DAVID WRIGHT (WRIGHT)

Today we're talking with Suzanne Updegraff. There are so many instances in each of our careers where we throw away our success through unprofessional behavior. Knowing the right tools to employ to create a powerful image, understanding how to develop a model for leadership performance, and aligning your personal goals through organizational results is imperative to getting ahead in today's fast-paced global economy. With etiquette as the essential core ingredient for enhancing your professionalism, this chapter will provide tips and proven techniques for adapting your style with your organization's culture. You'll also discover how to align your professional competencies with the strategic vision of your firm by implementing a defined model of behavior.

Suzanne welcome to *GPS for Success: Goals and Proven Strategies.*

SUZANNE UPDEGRAFF (UPDEGRAFF)

Thank you, David.

WRIGHT

How has our casual society influenced professional behavior in organizations?

UPDEGRAFF

Today's global business climate is much more casual in practice, and there are three broad dimensions affecting professional behavior in organizations.

The primary noticeable difference is seen in our professional dress and overall appearance. In the past, the corporate uniform was more defined and easier to identify.

Changes in societal and global trends dictate a more relaxed manner of working, and this method of behaving corresponds to how individuals are dressing.

Human Resource professionals are often interested in how to redirect an employee's inappropriate clothing or appearance. When I review their policy manual, it's discouraging to note that descriptive language regarding business-appropriate attire is almost non-existent or lacks specific meaning for an employee. Business casual attire is often the directive for employees and managers, and the interpretation is misunderstood and vague.

Dress, hygiene, and appearance are important elements that help define one's professional image and should not be minimized. Individuals are often promoted and/or overlooked for a promising position based upon clothing decisions, hairstyles, and attention to grooming.

The second dimension involves our casual approach to business relationships. Employees often find themselves revealing too many intimate details about their lives and are much more familiar with peers and management today. Because of this trend, more personal data is shared at work

It's not uncommon to learn details about co-workers on social networking sites, and the societal fabric of what data to share in a business setting has changed due to technology. We're not quite sure of what is appropriate to reveal when chatting with internal clients, and we're often unaware of how too much information about our personal lives can damage our professional reputations.

The third piece of how our casual society has influenced professional behavior is in the basic communication skills we employ. Technology has affected this dimension, but it's much more complex than cell phone usage or texting versus writing someone a business letter. We're much more casual in how we speak and the language we use. It's not uncommon to hear slang references, even when speaking with senior management or clients.

WRIGHT

Do generational differences influence professional behavior and what is the effect on professional etiquette?

UPDEGRAFF

Each generation brings its own unique communication and behavioral style when individuals enter the professional workforce. Technology punctuates generational differences and unfortunately, Generation Y (individuals born between 1979–2000) is often labeled as unprofessional because of misuse of electronic communication. Using technology in a corporate meeting while your manager is speaking is unprofessional because you aren't listening. Unfortunately, we tend to blame the technology, but the obvious offense is not paying attention to what is being discussed.

Another example of how the different generational issues influence professional behavior is in our understanding of working hours and a daily structure. A sophisticated, technological, global society dictates a different, more flexible flow for accomplishing tasks. Different generations embrace this more relaxed method in various ways and interpret one method as more professional than another. At the end of the day, business is about results; how those results are achieved is often viewed as either professional or not.

Understanding and having a strong knowledge base about what each generation might need in arriving at business solutions is important and involves competent communication skills.

WRIGHT

The word "etiquette" implies a less modern approach to conducting business. How will understanding and utilizing the correct use of etiquette help me in my career?

UPDEGRAFF

Wikipedia defines "etiquette" as a particular conduct or procedure defined by standards of measurement established in a particular culture. Etiquette is practiced by all of us each day, but can be misused when we lack adequate knowledge about how to employ the standard correctly.

Your performance during a business meeting can define your understanding or lack of understanding about meeting protocol. Accepted standards of conduct are part of the code that's referenced in the above definition. These standards might include not interrupting while others are speaking or knowing when to disagree with a client or executive. Becoming more sophisticated and polished in your etiquette during meetings will help define you as a more professional person.

Etiquette knowledge can enhance your career because you stand out as someone who knows how to behave appropriately.

Knowing the correct way to introduce one individual to another is a necessary skill that can be learned and will be useful in your business career. Proper etiquette gives you confidence and you appear more professionally competent.

WRIGHT

What are the obstacles to practicing and utilizing professional etiquette day-to-day in business?

UPDEGRAFF

One obstacle is lack of knowledge. We simply aren't aware of etiquette rules and are confused about the correct way to behave in certain situations. Our fast-paced society has presented obstacles with regard to polite interaction. We're multitasking while engaging with other individuals hundreds of times a day. This increases our stress levels; when your stress levels go up, the amount of polite ways of speaking and listening decrease.

Another obstacle to using proper etiquette is our long-term familiarity with colleagues and clients. Many individuals work for long periods of time within organizations, and the feeling of family is heightened when this occurs. Displaying behaviors that are normally reserved for your home and relatives is not uncommon. We begin to loosen up, we share information and intimacies, and we say and do things we would normally reserve for our more private relationships.

In today's casual world, many individuals aren't exposed to the proper way of doing things. We take a "fast-food" approach to behavior, communication, dining, and interacting and the message is one of apathy, ignorance, and unconcern.

WRIGHT

Would it be proper etiquette for me to ask how someone would like to be addressed and communicated with?

UPDEGRAFF

Absolutely. Respecting another person's preferred mode of communication is always a professional choice. Additionally, I've worked with clients who complain that their managers or peers have given them a nickname they didn't want. This is an example of an unprofessional habit.

WRIGHT

Will you provide for our readers an example of how an individual has used professionalism and expert etiquette to advance in his or her career or to even become more successful?

UPDEGRAFF

There is an old saying, "dress for the job you want, not the job you have." The same applies to communication, behavior, and etiquette understanding. If my intention were to advance in my career, I would immediately notice how senior management communicates and behaves. I might find a role model or mentor inside the organization who is considered a top-notch professional. Changing noticeable aspects of your performance can help you advance in your career.

I often share a simple story about one client who ate lunch at his desk each day. His manager viewed him as a less sophisticated professional because he didn't appear to have a work or refreshment balance. There was the additional problem of food smells surrounding his desk consistently. When my client began leaving the building for lunch and stopped eating at his desk, he gained a more professional appearance and image. Executives rarely eat at their desks, and when they do practice this, they normally have their own office and can dine in private.

Meeting deadlines, improving your posture, eliminating the slang references from your speech, and removing sarcastic remarks from your daily banter are all small examples of behaviors that will help advance your career.

One client wanted to change his image from that of "class-clown" to a more serious professional. He didn't completely adjust his personality overnight, but eliminated a bit of the joking to enhance a more professional demeanor.

Becoming more professional and embracing proper etiquette elevates your career to a higher level.

WRIGHT

What are some practices with regard to professionalism and etiquette that you consider non-negotiable in business?

UPDEGRAFF

I'll share what I consider to be the top five:

1. *Sharing too much personal information about yourself or your family.*
   Revealing intimate details places you over the invisible line marked Unprofessional Behavior. Your clients, co-workers, and members of management do not need to know the balance on your home mortgage. Your teenager's misbehavior last weekend is not necessary to share inside a professional climate. Sharing small tidbits about your past can also label you as unprofessional or immature.

2. *Your use of language can define you in terms of your background and education.*

   Cursing and using slang references are all viewed as unprofessional.

3. *Not returning telephone calls and not meeting deadlines is non-negotiable.*

   Internal and external clients expect you to perform, and when calls and e-mail messages are disregarded, you are viewed as someone who doesn't care.

4. *Displaying a lack of emotional intelligence is a sign of low self-control.*

   Using anger or rude behavior toward another person is always uncomfortable. It's never professional, even when it's justified and always looks, feels, and sounds ugly. We've all witnessed someone displaying anger and we don't enjoy it, even when we're not on the receiving end. Displaying any sort of strong emotion is a non-negotiable.

5. *Know, practice, and use proper table manners.*

   If you don't know the proper way to eat a piece of bread, find out. Don't assume that you practice all of the correct table skills. This is one area of professionalism that is often the most misunderstood and speaks volumes about your background and education.

WRIGHT

How important is the culture of an organization to achieving a professional reputation?

UPDEGRAFF

Cultural comprehension affects our long-term enjoyment of a job. Your professional reputation is enhanced when you blend with the culture, when you like the culture and the culture likes you, and when your style compliments the organization's strategic objectives.

I recently interviewed the manager of a large, well-known department store. The interviewee was incredibly focused on the service philosophies of her employer. She embraced the corporate culture and the values the company is known for in her conversation, her consistent smile, and in her positive energy when describing her routine day.

If an organizational culture doesn't complement your talents and strengths, you'll know quickly, and making the decision to move on should be immediate in order to deliver your best performance.

WRIGHT

You suggest that people's competence is their trademark. How can people change or enhance their competence to adjust their perceived trademark inside an organization?

UPDEGRAFF

David, when I began researching etiquette and professional behavior over a decade ago, the substantive piece missing from professional discussions surrounded the topic of competence. Obviously, if you're not competent you can't keep your job for very long, and your competence becomes your trademark or brand inside a firm. The most significant answer I hear when asking others about the most professional person they've ever known is a profound level of competence. Professionals know how to do their jobs, and they never stop learning.

Building your competence is so easy. Reading books, listening to educational material, attending workshops, and continuing your education through informal and formal coursework are all competence enhancers. Find out what your organization is doing by visiting its Web site once a week. Go to your favorite search engine and learn what the world sees when people search for your organization's name. Have lunch with a senior executive and ask questions. Talk with other departmental members and discover what they're working on that might affect your job. Memorize the mission, vision, and values of your firm. These small tips alone will help you appear more competent.

Begin learning more about your clients and find out what's important to them. Apply critical thinking to solutions and become more innovative in your approach to your day-to-day delivery of information. Step outside your comfort zone and practice a skill that might make you uncomfortable, but will enhance your career and knowledge base.

WRIGHT

Your work includes a model of behavior for professionalism. What is included in the model and how was the model developed?

UPDEGRAFF

In writing my book and developing the content for my workshops, I had to define what was most relevant for today's workforce with regard to understanding the importance of professional behavior. I also wanted to differentiate my material from the hundreds of resources available for a stronger etiquette understanding. I wanted the model to be useful enough to practice day-to-day, yet complex enough for those in my audience to grow in their careers.

The model is based upon societal trends that affect us in real-time, but provide core foundational pieces to separate us from competitors. My firm's expertise surrounds communication and behavior change, and the model for *Professional Presence in a Casual World* embraces these competencies. Behaviors are significant because others see your actions and habits; they hear your semantics and use of language and immediately create an image of you. The first piece of the model surrounds changing your behavior and communication to enhance your professional image.

The second step in the *Professional Presence in a Casual World* Model is your personal presentation. This includes your dress, grooming, appearance, and your personal style. This is a vibrant piece of the Model because we are often judged by our personal attributes. This step is particularly important if you are re-entering the work force or wanting to move forward in your chosen career. It's important to remember that before you give a presentation, you are a presentation.

The third piece is what I call "Business Presence," which encompasses your courtesies, manners, and your use of trust or confidential information. If I happen to share private information with you about an organizational decision and you keep my confidence, my image of you as a professional increases. Your business presence affects your relationships, your personal power, how you use politics, your understanding of the corporate culture, and how you behave in meetings.

WRIGHT

You've developed a professional model of behavior, but how can individuals adapt your model to customize a plan of action for their success?

UPDEGRAFF

You first have to be aware of what needs to change with your professional practices. I don't know anyone who doesn't need to change something about his or her behavior, communication style, appearance, or performance. Developing a healthy awareness about these professional elements and changing them accordingly will enhance your success.

Taking action requires you to think about particular areas where you feel less professional than you'd like. How limited is your knowledge about a particular subject? Where are you missing the mark? How do you behave in meetings? Do you remember a time, David, where perhaps you said something in front of peers and went home thinking, "I wish I hadn't said that"?

WRIGHT

Absolutely, probably within the last seven days.

UPDEGRAFF

Self-evaluation can help you apply the model for performance and behavior change, but other individuals can give you this gift, too.

An annual performance evaluation is a professional tool designed to help you learn about changes for greater success. Instead of becoming defensive when hearing what needs to change, use the information as a gift. Return to the Model described in Professional Presence in a Casual World and devote time to changing a particular area.

Ask trusted colleagues to also share with you something they've witnessed that might take away from your image. This is harder to practice, but can be invaluable in learning others' opinions of your daily habits.

WRIGHT

How do you define professionalism and etiquette for those who are unclear about their meaning and can you provide examples of each?

UPDEGRAFF

There are three definitions used interchangeably when describing a more professional approach to our work.

1. *Professionalism* is the conduct, aims, and qualities that characterize a person working in the business world. An example of professional behavior is not providing too many details when delivering an executive overview to a manager or group of senior individuals. Professional behavior dictates that you keep remarks concise when speaking to this audience.
2. *Manners* are social behaviors dictated by a particular group or society. Table manners are social behaviors with established, rich traditions. An example of exhibiting appropriate table manners is an understanding of where your bread and butter plate is located when dining at a business function. Another example is having knowledge about where to place your napkin if you must leave the table for a few minutes.
3. *Etiquette* is the conduct or procedure defined by standards of measurement established in a particular culture. Etiquette is displayed when you practice polite behavior toward another person. Opening doors, entering an elevator after others have departed the elevator, and properly addressing an individual are examples of etiquette practice.

WRIGHT

What trends in the workplace will affect professionalism and etiquette in the next few years?

UPDEGRAFF

There are three immediate trends influencing tomorrow's workforce:

1. *An understanding about global diversity is more than a trend.* Communicating and behaving with different cultures and understanding the particular nuances with regard to global appropriateness are imperative for tomorrow's professional.

2. *Using technology in an expert way.* Strengthen your competency with regard to how technology is advancing, but remember that different generations use technology in more diverse ways. A professional will provide a comfortable approach with technology use for the other person, particularly if you are dealing with a client.

3. *A greater focus on personal accountability is being exhibited throughout the corporate world.* When you examine the foundation of any firm, you're looking at the actions of the individuals who perform. When we're accountable for our mistakes and when we're accountable for our behavior, we become more professional. We each have a greater social responsibility to others and practicing professionalism in all contexts creates stronger relationships inside organizations.

WRIGHT

What a great conversation, and what an important one. I have the feeling that the underlying core here is just being polite and nice to people—how we dress, how we treat each other, the way we talk to each other, sharing too much information, the language that we use, not returning phone calls, not meeting deadlines, and nice table manners. It all seems like common sense, but when you put it all together it really is professional behavior.

UPDEGRAFF

Professional behavior is about practice. It shows up in all of the ways you engage others each day.

WRIGHT

I really do appreciate all this time you've taken today, Suzanne, to discuss this important subject and answering my questions. I really have learned a lot today and I'm sure that our readers will also.

UPDEGRAFF

David, thank you so much for your time. I've enjoyed chatting with you.

WRIGHT

Today we've been talking with Suzanne Updegraff. She believes and teaches how knowing the right tools to employ to create a powerful image, understanding how to develop a model for leadership performance, and aligning your personal goals with organizational results are all imperative to getting ahead in today's fast-paced global economy. I tend to believe her, too.

Suzanne, thank you so much for being with us today on *GPS for Success: Goals and Proven Strategies.*

UPDEGRAFF

You're welcome, David, thank you.

About the Author

Suzanne Updegraff is President of Employee Development Systems, a thirty-year-old performance improvement firm. Suzanne drives the vision and strategy of her firm. Her entertaining and engaging teaching style appeals to a diverse clientele ranging from corporate executives to individual contributors. Suzanne's success is crafted on personal attention, an interactive learning approach, and a sincere desire to transfer skill development and performance improvement for today's professional. Author of the publication, *Professional Presence in a Casual World,* Suzanne Updegraff has a proven track record for developing executive performance in individuals nationwide. Listed in the Denver Social Register, Suzanne is a member of Women's Vision Foundation, the American Society of Training & Development, as well as Society of Human Resource Management. She is married with two children and resides in Denver, Colorado.

Suzanne Updegraff
Employee Development Systems, Inc.
Dry Creek Business Park
7308 South Alton Way, Suite 2J
Centennial, CO 80112